Carve Your Life

Enduring Wisdom: From a Father to his son

"It is better to learn from other's mistakes, rather committing yourself and learn".

Wing Commander
Vikas Raghav

BLUEROSE PUBLISHERS
India | U.K.

Copyright © Wing Commander Vikas Raghav 2024

All rights reserved by author. No part of this publication may be reproduced, stored in a retrieval system or transmitted in any form or by any means, electronic, mechanical, photocopying, recording or otherwise, without the prior permission of the author. Although every precaution has been taken to verify the accuracy of the information contained herein, the publisher assumes no responsibility for any errors or omissions. No liability is assumed for damages that may result from the use of information contained within.

BlueRose Publishers takes no responsibility for any damages, losses, or liabilities that may arise from the use or misuse of the information, products, or services provided in this publication.

For permissions requests or inquiries regarding this publication, please contact:

BLUEROSE PUBLISHERS
www.BlueRoseONE.com
info@bluerosepublishers.com
+91 8882 898 898
+4407342408967

ISBN: 978-93-6452-347-9

Cover Design: Sadhna Kumari
Typesetting: Pooja Sharma

First Edition: August 2024

DEDICATED TO

My dear son Vijayant, I dedicate this book to you with the utmost pride and love. The pages within hold a treasury of my life experiences and hard-earned insights, all crafted to illuminate the path for aspiring young professionals like you as they embark on their journey into the world of professionals.

Just as life mirrors the undulating pattern of a sine wave, with its crests and troughs signifying the joys and challenges, this book strives to capture the richness of such experiences.

Not only is this an acknowledgement of the individuals who have graced my professional and personal odyssey, but it also embodies the invaluable teachings garnered from the profound tapestry of both astute and misguided decisions. I dedicate this book to all those who have been part of my journey as a working professional and as an individual. It also represents all the valuable lessons I've learnt from both my wise and foolish decisions.

ABOUT THE BOOK

Life is indeed complex and becomes even more intricate if we don't make the right decisions to shape it beautifully. Despite its complexity, life offers us countless opportunities, and seizing them at the right moment can genuinely make a difference. "Carve Your Life" is a guide for Young Professionals. It is an incredibly comprehensive book designed to help young professionals navigate the intricacies of the modern world. Drawing from the author's personal experiences and practical insights, this book offers a roadmap for establishing a balanced and fulfilling life right from the beginning of one's career.

This book covers essential aspects of life, including work, financial management, married life, and fitness. It provides insights on excelling in careers, setting goals, maintaining work-life balance, achieving financial stability, nurturing relationships, and promoting physical and mental well-being.

"Carve Your Life" offers empowering anecdotes and practical advice to help young professionals take charge of their lives. It serves as a reliable companion, providing guidance on aspects such as finance, family, and health, to foster success and fulfillment in both professional and personal spheres.

Let "Carve Your Life" be the guiding light for young professionals so that they can navigate challenges and strive to build a life that is not only successful but also meaningful and enriching. Making the right choices at the beginning of career can greatly simplify and balance life.

ABOUT THE AUTHOR

Wing Commander Vikas Raghav is a distinguished officer in the Indian Air Force with over 25 years of exemplary service. Hailing from a modest background and growing up in a middle-class family, he has worked diligently to ascend to esteemed roles, including Commanding Officer, Senior Instructor, and Chief Operations Officer. His extensive experience includes air defence operations, administration, and human resource management, showcasing his multifaceted expertise and dedication to service.

Wing Commander Vikas Raghav has written his first self-help book for young professionals, offering valuable insights and practical advice on balancing work-life demands, personal growth, financial management, and maintaining physical fitness. His book reflects his passion for mentoring and guiding the next generation through the complexities of modern life.

In his remarkable career, Wing Commander Vikas Raghav has consistently shown strong leadership and resilience. He has always demonstrated unwavering commitment, professionalism and integrity. His insights, gained from many years of experience in high-pressure environments, form a solid foundation for the guidance he provides through his writing.

Wing Commander Vikas Raghav is accomplished professionally and a strong advocate for creative thinking, continuous learning, and self-improvement. His dedication to personal development and assisting others in reaching their potential is evident in his thoughtful and practical approach to life's challenges.

Wing Commander Vikas Raghav inspires, embodying discipline, perseverance, and compassion. He has penned an empowering debut book to guide young professionals towards leading more fulfilling lives. Through his insightful work, he seeks to inspire early adjustments in their careers and personal lives, paving the way for a positively impactful future.

SINCERE THANKS TO

I sincerely appreciate the invaluable help and unwavering support extended to me by my dear friend Nidhi Juyal and my sister Supriya in reviewing this book. Their sustained encouragement has been absolutely pivotal to my journey. Nidhi and Supriya, your guidance has illuminated my path, assuring me that my words would not only resonate but also touch lives.

I extend my heartfelt gratitude to my daughter Amishi (Mishi) for her invaluable assistance with publicity and social media marketing. Amishi, your efforts have significantly contributed to the success of this book, and I am truly grateful to you for your support.

To my son Vijayant (Viji), I express my sincere thanks for being such an honest and obedient son. Viji, your sincerity has inspired me to provide you with unwavering support and guidance. This book stands as a small token of my contribution to your life.

I am profoundly grateful to all my friends, adversaries, colleagues, subordinates, superiors and bosses who have been part of my life, both personally and professionally. Their presence and interactions have not only enriched my life but also shaped my writing journey, and for that, I am truly thankful to them.

Last but certainly not least, my deepest thanks to my wife Kalpana for her unwavering support throughout the writing process. Kalpana, your encouragement and reassurance steered me in the right direction even when I shared my unedited work with you.

PROLOGUE

The pronoun "he" in this book is used generically to refer to individuals of any gender. There is no gender bias, and my intended audience is young professionals who are just starting their careers. Although the lessons in this book are applicable at any stage of life, they are most beneficial for young professionals.

As children progress through various stages of education, from school to college, they often find themselves in need of guidance. These transitions can be challenging, marking the end of carefree days and the beginning of a more demanding academic journey. With each passing year, studies and responsibilities increase, and life becomes more complex, particularly around the age of 15 or 16.

Children are responsible for choosing their careers and selecting professional streams in college based on their capabilities and interests. Many young students struggle with this decision, often influenced by current trends, their peers' choices, or their parents' unfulfilled dreams. Parental pressure plays a significant role, as parents want their children to succeed in areas where they may have struggled in the past.

In many instances, children often lack adequate guidance in making informed career decisions, leading to many of them choosing career paths without a comprehensive understanding or genuine personal choice. This frequently results in challenges such as college dropouts and struggles within their chosen professions.

Amidst the trials and tribulations, there lies a silver lining of personal growth. Even when circumstances seem to dictate our career paths, we still hold the power to steer our lives towards positive change through unwavering effort and resilience. **Life is a series of opportunities, and it's our ability to seize them at the right moment that truly matters**.

Choosing a career is a journey that can be approached in two distinct ways. The first method involves making a thoughtful decision based on personal skills, interests, and desires. The alternative route entails making a choice based on prevailing circumstances and committing wholeheartedly to it. While the likelihood of pursuing the former path is rather slim, committing to the chosen career path, nurturing a keen interest, and diligently investing effort are not just important, but they are the keys to unlocking success.

This book is not designed to offer career counselling but to provide guidance for soon-to-graduate young scholars at universities or young professionals, aiding them in carving their professional lives. Whether career choices are deliberate or detailed, the primary goal of this book is to equip individuals with the foundational knowledge necessary to thrive in any profession, encompassing both professional and general life skills.

In military life, I have noticed, upon joining military stations after training, numerous young officers find it challenging to maintain a healthy equilibrium between their professional responsibilities and personal lives. Some officers are drawn to military service by its glamorous external image, only to discover the inherent challenges. This phenomenon is not exclusive to military life, as many professions may exude attraction from a distance but individuals find them different when they join that profession. For individuals to excel in their careers, focusing on their chosen path, diligently learning their professional duties, and sustaining unwavering focus are crucial.

It's essential to focus on developing our professional skills, but it's also crucial to understand the broader aspects of life. Many of us need guidance in areas such as finance, family, and health as we progress in our careers. While we often learn from our failures and by observing others, having early guidance can significantly impact our professional and personal development. This doesn't mean we should be guided through our entire professional life, but a bit of support at the start of a career can make a big difference. Ultimately, we all learn from our mistakes and experiences; however, learning from the mistakes of others can save us from unnecessary pain and setbacks.

Looking back at my own life and career, I wish I had someone to guide me in carving my professional, personal, and financial life. I believe that with the proper guidance, I could have achieved more. Now, I see similar challenges young professionals face, so my goal is to help them carve their lives and destinies. I want to assist them in various aspects of their lives so that they can become responsible and successful individuals.

A LETTER TO MY SON,

12 Oct 22/ 1600 hr

My Dear Vijayant,

After my afternoon nap, I sat waiting for my cup of coffee, with a mix of drowsiness and wakefulness. I found myself reflecting on my past achievements and mistakes. These thoughts provoked an analysis of my successes and failures. I realised that **we are not robots** that can be fine-tuned by updating the latest software. I realised that, **as humans, we are not perfect and are bound to make mistakes**. We are constantly learning and adapting based on our experiences. We update our "software" by observing and learning from our surroundings and from the people in our lives. By paying attention to the actions and behaviours of our parents, siblings, friends, and environment, we can gain valuable lessons and insights to help us improve.

I see, you are about to enter the professional world after completing your B.Tech (Computer Science) degree. Transitioning from college to a professional environment can bring new challenges and experiences. As professionals, our lives differ from what they were like in college. Work-life offers us different challenges and peculiarities that we never faced during college. From a relaxed and calm student, we sometimes join a professional field full of challenges and we don't realise how to start life and move on. I wish you a great career with lots of success and fame, but let me caution you that life is challenging outside college.

The trajectory of work-life is not a simple straight line but rather a complex zigzag line. On one end, work-life offers independence, while on the other end, there are responsibilities and complexities due to various factors. Success for a student is achievable through hard work, dedication, and sincerity towards their studies. The level of intelligence has less impact than the commitment to studies. Even a student with an average IQ can excel with hard work, focus, and sincerity. College life is about the amount of late-night studying done (rather than staying up late to watch FIFA or IPL).

Life can be more complicated as a professional than as a student. **If you make the right choices at the beginning of your career, you can simplify and balance out your life to a large extent.** However, your professional life and your choices regarding workplace relations, financial management, marriage, physical fitness, and ambition will carve your life for better or worse.

I've experienced ups and downs, successes and failures, smiles and sorrows, all because of my good and bad choices. **Always remember your life is a reflection of your choices. You carve your life, good or bad, successful or disastrous, purely by your choices.**

At this point, you may think that becoming a computer science engineer is the most challenging job, but remember that you are at a comfortable stage in your life. Your journey of struggles is yet to begin. Even though working in the Indian Air Force is a different ball game, the fundamentals in the workplace and personal life will remain more or less the same as they are in civil world. I want to share life lessons from the journey of my personal and professional odyssey with you.

My professional environment and work culture stand in sharp contrast to civil domains. My workplace is characterised by an atmosphere of exhilaration and high stakes, where split-second decision-making is the norm and life-and-death scenarios are a regular part of air battles. The adrenaline-fueled excitement, thrill, and intense pressure make each day unique and demanding.

In the armed forces, particularly in aerial combat, individuals gain invaluable insights and skills that extend far beyond their time in service. They are immersed in high-stakes, life-and-death scenarios that demand accurate decision-making, a heightened sense of responsibility, and the ability to think innovatively and creatively. The complexities inherent in these situations can profoundly shape individuals, either bolstering their capabilities or leading to instant setbacks. These experiences instill a deep understanding of the need to execute duties with the utmost precision, as individuals bear the weight of responsibility for themselves, their organisation, and their Nation as a whole.

The way you feel about your job is closely tied to your interactions with your organisation, as well as with your superiors, coworkers, and subordinates. I have personally experienced how my bosses, colleagues, and subordinates have impacted my life. The decisions made and the relationships formed in the workplace significantly influence one's life and can greatly affect career advancement and overall well-being.

Throughout my 25 years of professional experience as an operations head, administrator, and leader, I have encountered various challenging situations that have imparted invaluable life lessons. Upon reflection, I take satisfaction in approaching life with a mindful perspective and consistently prioritising the goals of the organisations I've been a part of. However, there were instances where I could have exercised more tact and diplomacy in managing certain situations.

Life is full of ups and downs, navigating through narrow, broad, and twisted lanes. It is sometimes possible to deal with life situations on the front foot; sometimes, one might have to take a few steps back, and sometimes, one might have to duck down. I often get a feeling about a few things; alas, if only I had done that particular thing differently, or maybe if I had controlled my emotions at that time, or perhaps if I could have waited to make that decision after two days... maybe... maybe... maybe... there are so many maybe (s).

If given the opportunity, I would like to repair many rough patches in my life, but that won't be possible. **The least I can do is sharing my experiences with you and teach you a few lessons I have learnt in life.**

My personal and professional past evokes mixed feelings in me, but I understand that I cannot change it. I am documenting these experiences as lessons learnt and aiming to impart these lessons to you and other young professionals.

In the span of 25 years in my professional career and nearly 48 years on this planet, I have had the opportunity to observe the intricate tapestry of life closely. From the highs and lows of marriage and parenthood to navigating dynamic relationships with both exceptional and challenging bosses, friends, and colleagues, I have encountered a wide array of experiences. Along the way, I have faced favourable and challenging circumstances, including financial hardship. I have learnt valuable lessons from significant mistakes, particularly in economic and human management, impacting my life journey.

The best I can do is giving you a few tips based on my experiences so that you can avoid some mistakes. While I can't promise you a perfect life, I'm confident that you'll have an easier journey if you pay close attention to my advice. My suggestions may not be groundbreaking, but they are practical and achievable.

In our complex and diverse world, it's natural to encounter a wide range of situations at work and in our personal lives. We aspire to achieve success and reach our full potential, whether through dedication and hard work or employing alternative strategies. While you may not face the same challenges I have encountered, and I sincerely hope that you don't have to confront similar difficulties. There are valuable lessons to learn from these experiences that can empower you to enhance your life. Let me now take the opportunity to share the insights and wisdom I've gained along the way.

CONTENTS

ABOUT THE BOOK v
ABOUT THE AUTHOR vii
PROLOGUE xi
A LETTER TO MY SON, ... xv
1. YOU MAKE THE WORKPLACE – CHAOTIC OR LOVABLE 1
2. LET'S CREATE WEALTH 49
3. FINDING SENORITA OR SENOR 112
4. ADDITIONAL CHAPTER 21 Jul 23/ 2010 hr 132
5. FITNESS: THE ULTIMATE TREASURE 143
6. CONCLUDING CHAPTER 181
ANNEXURE TO CHAPTER 5 188
REFERENCES 193

CHAPTER 1

YOU MAKE THE WORKPLACE – CHAOTIC OR LOVABLE

Life at Work Place

Throughout our professional careers, we are required to assume multiple roles in the workplace. These roles include subordinate, colleague, and boss, each demanding different approaches, interactions, skills, and emotional intelligence. While we may predominantly play one role at a time, it's common to fulfill multiple roles simultaneously. For instance, early in our careers, we often act as subordinates while collaborating with colleagues. As we progress, we may take on supervisory responsibilities, requiring us to balance the roles of boss, colleague, and subordinate. In the initial years, focusing on learning, building strong relationships, and contributing to the organisation's growth is crucial. As we advance, we may find ourselves in leadership positions, necessitating a different approach in managing these multiple roles.

We take on different roles in life, such as son, father, friend, or guide. Similarly, we assume various roles in our professional life. While we are often taught how to interact with bosses and colleagues, learning how to work with subordinates is equally important. It's essential to embody leadership qualities from the beginning of our professional lives, regardless of our position in the organisation. Leadership skills are valuable at every stage of life.

Selecting Work-Life

It's essential to carefully consider your options before choosing your first company or workplace. Both government and corporate jobs have their advantages and disadvantages. Government jobs offer stability but limited individual growth. It can be challenging to drive change within the organisation at a fast pace in government jobs. On the other hand, corporate jobs are fast-paced and often recognise talent quickly. Energy and talent are rewarded with promotions and financial benefits in corporate jobs. However, corporate jobs lack the stability and security provided by government positions.

The question is: What kind of company or organisation should one start their professional career with? Many of us seek jobs with good perks, privileges, and attractive salaries at this stage. Friends, family, and relatives often pressure us to find a job with a good reputation and high pay. Even when we choose our career path after high school, it's usually due to peer, family, or friend pressure rather than a well-considered decision. As a result, some Engineers and Doctors pursue careers as guitarists, artists, yoga teachers, spiritual gurus, or even restaurant owners or entrepreneurs after completing their degrees. Only a few of us clearly know what we want to become after high school. Our education system and professional course selection processes are based on something other than skills. In some cases, individuals who decide to pursue a career in business administration may not be thoroughly assessed for traits or interests specific to business administration. Before selection, we are tested for one thing and taught something else. Most of us don't choose our careers based on our skill sets; we base our choices on current trends and social pressures.

So, now what to do? How can we change the system? You will say you are already on the path to become a computer science engineer. What can you do now? How can you find your calling?

Don't worry; I am not asking you to start looking for your calling and change your life based on your calling or desires. No, you can't afford to do so now. Neither you nor other students of your age should make such a change at this stage. Some students give up due to the pressures of studies and quit studying to change streams. Some, relatively a few, could only sense they were made for something else and had to give up everything to pursue their dream work/ job.

There is a beautiful Japanese concept known as "IKIGAI," which helps in identifying one's calling. Let me just briefly explain the IKIGAI[i] concept to you. This Japanese concept is about the conglomeration of four key elements in life, viz.

What you LOVE

What the WORLD NEEDS

What you can be PAID FOR

What you are GOOD AT

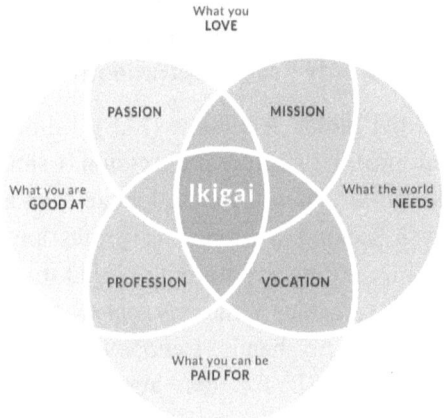

Recognising one's own capabilities and choosing a professional career can be incredibly rewarding. However, discovering one's passion at a young age is often challenging. It involves identifying activities that bring joy, which can sometimes be difficult due to immaturity and inexperience. Determining one's strengths and focusing on skill development is a simpler first step. The next step, identifying a calling that positively impacts, both your own life and the lives of others, is more complex. Finally, it is not easy to earn a livelihood through your skills while bringing joy and impact to other's life.

If all four elements of life can be found in one place, it becomes a person's IKIGAI, or 'Purpose of Life.' The concept of IKIGAI is excellent for identifying what one would like to do on the basis of its four key elements. However, it's not easy to sit and identify these elements within oneself and decide on one's future. Discovering the balance of these four elements takes a lot of effort. Indian cricketer MS Dhoni is an example of someone who discovered his IKIGAI and pursued it. Only a few people, like MS Dhoni, get the opportunity to prove themselves in their desired fields. It's important to remember that we often see the success of individuals like MS Dhoni in hindsight. It's like looking at the past performance of stocks or mutual funds and saying, "If only we had bought this stock ten years ago, we would have made 100 million by now. **Exceptions cannot be replicated; we can only draw inspiration from them**.

When I joined the Indian Air Force (IAF), I didn't know much about my work profile or career progression. I simply wanted to be a FAUJI (a military man) because I came from a middle-class family and was seeking a promising profession with a good salary. It was only during my training period that I learnt about my work profile. At that point, my only option was to start loving what I had in my hands. I chose to make my work and profession 'my IKIGAI' for two reasons. First, leaving a government job due to a contract was difficult, and second, I needed a reputable job. My best option was to cultivate an interest in whatever I had. I firmly believe that **there is nothing that one cannot learn with sincerity and hard work**.

I began my professional journey in the Indian Air Force, which I consider my IKIGAI. Many of us fail to appreciate what we already have and spend our lives in pursuit of something greater. **It's important to remember that nothing works unless you dedicate time and energy to it.** Even opening a general store requires time, energy, sincerity, and hard work to make it successful. MS Dhoni didn't become a cricketer overnight. He was focused, confident in his dreams and abilities, and, most importantly, willing to face failure. Here's another lesson I've learnt from observing successful people. Those who have 'little to lose' but possess talent, focus, and determination can succeed with hard work and sincerity. They have fewer fears of failure as they don't have much to lose. Of course, being skilled is the first requirement. If you look at successful cricketers, singers, entrepreneurs, or professionals in any field, you'll notice that those who are willing to bet their lives on their dreams become successful sooner or later. Focus, skill, hard work, and sincerity will always be essential for a successful career.

It's essential to consider your Computer Science Engineering profession as your IKIGAI, at least for now. Let's continue our discussion about choosing your first company. It's crucial to prioritise learning and gaining experience in your first job over focusing solely on salary packages. The best company for you is one that provides a solid foundation, diverse exposure, new challenges and opportunities to learn new skills during the initial years of your career. Instead of being overly concerned about minor differences in salary, focus on developing your skills and expertise. If you have the right environment to apply your theoretical knowledge to practical work, success is inevitable. Your first company can significantly impact your career trajectory, a lesson I learnt while in the IAF. The Armed Forces infuse leadership skills and moral values from day one, offering exposure to various experiences across different branches and duty locations. Choosing a challenging work environment at the start of your career can provide valuable opportunities for learning and growth. Embrace challenges and seek out opportunities to enhance your skills. Look for a first company that offers broad exposure and ample learning opportunities.

First Day at Workplace

It's important to understand where to focus when defining your IKIGAI and selecting your job. It's crucial to realise that you may have little control over the situation at this stage. Whatever decision you make and whichever company you choose, stick to that for some time. When you start your first day at work, approach it with an open mind and positivity, as challenges will begin from this point onwards. The first day at the workplace is like making a first impression when meeting someone. It's essential to stay normal, but you may feel anxious, confused, and clueless. The key is to stay calm, as it's only the first day. You have your whole career ahead of you, so **take time to understand things on the first day instead of trying to prove yourself immediately**.

Remember to dress appropriately for your first day at work and bring all necessary documents. Approach everyone with an open mind and a smile, and listen carefully to your team leader or immediate boss. They may explain your tasks in a simple or complex manner, so try to understand as much as possible. It's okay to take your time to get up to speed with your work. Feel proud that you have been selected to work for this company, even if it's not your dream job. Remember that many people would love to be in your position. Some people start their new jobs complaining as if they were invited to join the company, but remember you chose to be here, so embrace this opportunity and enjoy your first day. Take small steps and find joy in your new professional journey.

As a boss, I always made sure to give my subordinates, especially the young officers who joined the station after their initial training, enough time to adjust themselves without explicitly expressing it. Despite appearing to put pressure on them, I actually expected very little from them for the first few months. This approach is generally common among bosses and team leaders. However, I always looked for certain qualities in young professionals, such as honesty, sincerity, a willingness to learn, and the ability to work hard. I am always pleased when I find someone focused on work and striving for excellence in profession, regardless of other factors.

When you start your career, you will likely be in a subordinate role. On your first day, dress your best and focus on observing and understanding your workplace, meeting your boss and colleagues. It's important to be well-dressed, have a pleasant demeanor, good manners, and strong communication skills. **Being good at your job is important, but having good communication skills, manners, and etiquette will make you stand out as a well-rounded professional and a gentleman**.

Core Work

As a subordinate, one must focus on their core job. After working a few days, it's important to start understanding and focusing on the core responsibilities. Working with sincerity, hard work, and the ability to achieve desired results in the expected time is crucial for subordinates. This is what brings recognition. **Blaming destiny or anything else for being weak in core work is not an option**. Destiny is not a factor; we create our success through hard work and skills. The word 'Destiny' is just an excuse for weak employees. **Staying focused and working hard on core responsibilities is the key to success**. This is the main attribute bosses look for, regardless of anything else. Even if you were average in college or training, it's crucial to concentrate and excel as a professional in your core work now. Your other qualities will complement your strong professional knowledge.

We all encounter opportunities and must seek them out through wisdom, determination, and perseverance. Let me give you an example. You didn't dream of studying engineering at PES University (one of the best in Bangalore); it wasn't destined for you. Instead, you created this opportunity for yourself through hard work. Think back to when you were in 12th grade. Were you the same person as you are today? No, you weren't. After your 12th-grade exams, you worked hard and took a break from regular studies to prepare for competitive exams. You took a chance, not knowing if you would succeed. Your decision-making at that young age has paid off. **We shouldn't wait for destiny to provide answers; we must carve our lives**. Every step you take can be critical in carving your life, so we need to make decisions consciously.

Working in a core job involves learning essential skills and addressing weaknesses. The ability to critically analyse one's shortcomings comes with experience. As a young employee (and later also), it's essential not to take offence when your work is criticised. Instead, take criticism as an opportunity for learning and improvement. It is okay to acknowledge areas where you can improve. **Identifying and working on your weaknesses will contribute to your success in the long run.** Once you know your weaknesses, list them and assess their impact on a scale of 1 to 10. Then, consciously prioritise and address them, starting with the most impactful ones.

Alongside your core work, honing soft skills such as analytical thinking, effective communication, and persuasive presentation can be instrumental in shaping your professional growth. When tackling an assignment, don't just rely on your core skills but also bring in sincerity, hard work, and in-depth analytical capability. Evaluate the strengths, weaknesses, opportunities, and threats (SWOT analysis) of the task and structure your work plan accordingly. Expressing your thoughts on the assignment preparation, even before initiating the work, can lead to more successful outcomes. The key point I want to stress is the significance of preparation. Before any crucial assignment or meeting, devote time to thorough preparation and be prepared for the unexpected. Anticipate potential questions that may arise during your presentation and arm yourself with answers. This level of preparation is a result of a comprehensive in-depth analysis of your core job.

Foundation Years (at least initial two years...)

Since day two at the office (after our initial conversation about staying calm on day one), it's crucial to be fully engaged for the next two years. This means dedicating yourself to your professional responsibilities around the clock. Your work should become a top priority in your life during this foundational period. Focus on building a solid expertise in your core work - give it your all, aiming for 200% effort. Strengthening this foundation will pave the way for smoother progress in the future. It's important to practice active listening, observation, and restraint in speaking, especially when engaging in potentially counterproductive arguments, particularly with your superiors.

As a young professional, it's essential to recognise and respect your boss's knowledge and experience, even if he is from the Stone Age and you are from the latest generation. While you may be well-versed in the latest technologies and trends, your boss's years of experience should not be discounted.

When it comes to sharing your opinions or arguments with your boss, it's not just important, it's essential to do so in a respectful and diplomatic manner. It's crucial to express your thoughts logically and sensitively without coming across as confrontational. Maintaining a pleasant demeanour and a friendly smile can help create a positive and collaborative atmosphere, fostering a sense of mutual respect and understanding.

The key is to present your arguments in a way that supports your perspective without undermining your boss's authority. It's essential to approach these interactions to contribute to the discussion rather than asserting your ego.

Ultimately, it's essential to remember that your boss carries the ultimate responsibility and likely possesses a deep understanding of the relevant facts and considerations. Therefore, it's natural for them to carefully evaluate and consider your arguments before making decisions.

Instead of trying to win your argument right away, it's better to take your time. Rather than insisting on winning immediately, it's more effective to set aside your strong desire to win and consider your boss's perspective. Take the time to analyse it thoroughly, refine your arguments, and present them later if you still believe you are right. In the meantime, carry out the work the way your boss wants. You can incorporate the results of the partially finished work into your future arguments.

In our professional lives, it's common to take pride in our skills and expertise, but sometimes, this pride can lead to overlooking the perspectives of others. It's essential to pause and consider different viewpoints before coming to conclusions, especially when interacting with supervisors and coworkers. Rather than dismissing their experiences, listening and understanding their perspectives can be highly valuable. Remember, it's not essential to rush to prove your point; instead, focus on building a strong case supported by knowledge and analytical capabilities. By taking the time needed to prepare, you can bolster your arguments and present them effectively.

The workplace can often be the site of conflicts between employees and their superiors, particularly when individuals have a strong and assertive nature. While engaging in professional discussions and debates is essential, ensuring these interactions are constructive is crucial. Rather than asserting oneself verbally, it is more impactful to demonstrate professionalism and expertise through the quality of one's work and output. When your competence and commitment to your work are evident, it becomes easier to avoid unnecessary arguments.

It's also important to recognise that some bosses may be driven by personal agendas shaped by their self-centered nature. These individuals may prioritise their interests above all else. In such situations, navigating and managing these relationships carefully is essential, ensuring that you can maintain professionalism and effectiveness in your work despite the challenges posed by such superiors.

Focus on Yourself

Remember that building lasting friendships in the workplace can be challenging due to the diverse interests of your colleagues, including your boss. This creates a competitive environment where you compete not only with your peers and superiors but also with your own previous achievements. Embracing continuous self-improvement is crucial, so make it a habit to enhance your skills and refine your personality regularly. Strive to evolve into a superior professional, communicator, and influencer by dedicating yourself to daily learning and gradual skill development.

During your early days at work, it's crucial to avoid falling into the trap of complacency by simply fulfilling routine tasks. Instead, take the initiative to seek out and seize significant opportunities. Aspire to become an exceptional leader and influencer in your field, understanding that these qualities can be acquired and cultivated through conscious effort. Therefore, focus on broadening your professional horizons and gaining a comprehensive understanding of your company's operations and industry by observing and learning from your superiors, colleagues, and subordinates.

Success in developing leadership skills is also dependent on your commitment to being a reputable and trustworthy professional. Always prioritise truthfulness and transparency in your interactions with your boss, colleagues, and subordinates. Strive to foster a supportive and productive workplace environment, steering clear of office politics. Your dedication to honesty, reliability, and sincerity will help you build a positive image that will earn the trust and respect of those around you.

Finally, guarding and nurturing your professional image is paramount. Continuously aim to outgrow your peers by setting high standards for yourself and striving to think and act at a level above your current position. This steadfast focus on personal growth will position you for success while contributing to your workplace's overall productivity and positive atmosphere.

Communication Skills

Understanding the essence of effective communication is essential for success in various aspects of life, particularly in leadership roles and conflict resolution. Developing strong communication skills empowers individuals to articulate their ideas and opinions respectfully, engage in constructive negotiations, and, above all, comprehend the perspectives and needs of others. Although both written and verbal communication skills are valuable, verbal communication skills hold a slightly higher level of importance. Proficient communicators are cognizant of their abilities and limitations, allowing them to anticipate and navigate the potential impact of their communication before conveying their message. Embracing the significance of practical communication skills can lead to a greater sense of purpose and facilitate deeper connections and empathy with individuals in your personal and professional spheres.

Finding Purpose and Core Competencies

It can be easy to talk about the importance of finding a purpose in life, but actually identifying a meaningful purpose can be challenging. This is particularly true when starting a new job, as work demands may take precedence over personal reflection. However, it's essential to gradually cultivate work stamina while contemplating the long-term outcomes you hope to achieve. Your ultimate goal or desired result can serve as your driving purpose. To determine this result, evaluating your core strengths and areas of passion is essential.

There are numerous examples where, even after learning a skill or gaining a professional degree, some people have changed their field of work and followed their instincts. Yes, it is possible, but first of all, you should know yourself and be aware of your strong and weak areas. Once you can identify your core competencies, you may choose to move ahead in life. Before changing your career, prepare well; don't leave your job or career based solely on instinct. Give yourself time to build on the alternative you are considering. You must do a SWOT analysis of your thoughts. You can decide once you have thoroughly thought about it and earned enough to take the risk.

If, after a few years, you still firmly believe you have other areas of interest based on your skills and desires, then by all means, pursue those interests. However, if you feel differently, it's essential to focus and develop your interest in your current field of work. Remember, gaining experience and saving money will allow you to change your field when the time is right. It's crucial to have the ability to turn our skills into our interests. Remember that changing your field of work is always possible based on the world's demands. It's worth noting that ordinary people live as the things come, but wise individuals take control and actively build their own lives. To achieve something significant, we must dedicate ourselves to the path we choose and be ready to seize the opportunities that come our way.

Learn the Art of Losing with Grace

There have been numerous instances in my professional experience where I found myself in situations where I attempted to convey important points to my superiors or make a case in meetings. Still, my suggestions and arguments were ignored or rejected. I felt unheard and often faced humiliation in front of others. Even though I was confident in the validity of my points, I often felt compelled to remain silent when the tides turned against me. However, with time, it became evident that my perspective was indeed valid. Such occurrences are not uncommon in the workplace, given individuals' diverse needs, aspirations, and viewpoints. It's crucial to remain patient when encountering criticism and facing situations where one's perspective is overlooked. It's only through experiencing setbacks that we can genuinely value our triumphs, as both victories and defeats are an integral part of life.

In life, there will be times when it may seem like you're facing setbacks and losing battles. Remember to stay patient and resilient, whether it is a temporary setback or a more permanent one. It's natural to experience failures or have your opinions overlooked or challenged, even when you know you're in the right. You don't need to win every battle on any given day. Instead, bide your time; the satisfaction of having your perspective acknowledged and accepted by many will be all the greater when it finally happens. A dedicated and hardworking approach cannot go unnoticed indefinitely. While there may be obstacles along the way, brighter days are sure to come. The key is perseverance. Through persistence, you will carve out a reputation for yourself. You'll be known as someone who doesn't speak unnecessarily and isn't quick to jump into disagreements. Your reputation will be built on a strong foundation of knowledge and depth, and your arguments will be firmly grounded in fact when you do present them. You'll earn this status by prevailing in some situations and remaining silent in others. If you're right, time will eventually affirm it.

When it comes to your interactions with your bosses, it's vital not to seek to outshine them. While you might occasionally prove them wrong, they, too, will have their moments. Some bosses may make it a point to prove you wrong if you attempt to outdo them. However, by maintaining a sincere, hardworking, and persevering approach, you will eventually earn your boss's respect and trust.

At times, individuals may find themselves becoming overly confident in their abilities, leading to egotistical behaviour. This excessive self-assurance can result in a tendency to persist in one's own viewpoint, even when it is unnecessary. It's crucial to consider the needs of the team and our role before articulating our arguments in a manner that upholds everyone's pride. Overconfidence and a lack of accurate self-assessment can be harmful. It's often more beneficial to listen attentively and speak judiciously. This approach allows for a better evaluation of any situation and reduces the likelihood of becoming overconfident or making misguided assessments of our capabilities.

By observing others, staying aware of our environment, and understanding the topic at hand, we can prepare ourselves for meetings or presentations. This heightened level of awareness is in line with the concept of situational awareness (SA) in aviation, which involves keen observation of our environment. Increased SA allows us to process information quickly, assess risk, make swift decisions, and confidently advocate for our positions, ultimately boosting our confidence. As a result, heightened SA sharpens our senses and strengthens our intuition.

We shouldn't let small failures or defeats in everyday discussions discourage us. We can reduce the likelihood of failure by staying focused and honing our ability to refine our arguments. It's important to remember that no one can make us feel humiliated unless we permit them to do so. Handling failures gracefully and using them as opportunities to bounce back and showcase our capabilities is essential. Sometimes, embracing failure is necessary to gain valuable lessons. In any situation, failures provide us with more profound insights than victories. Therefore, it's crucial to prioritise hard work and sincerity over the desire to win at all costs.

Alignment with the Objectives of the Organisation

Understanding our organisation's specific requirements and expectations is crucial for navigating our workplace effectively. Our decisions and behaviours are influenced by the depth of our knowledge and understanding of the organisation's dynamics. This underscores the importance of developing a strong foundation of expertise early in our careers. An inadequate understanding of our organisation can lead to misunderstandings and conflicts with our immediate superiors. Staying within the established direction and goals set by the organisation's leadership is vital. Aligning our professional skills and expertise with the organisation's overarching goals is essential, especially in the initial years of our careers. During this formative period, our supervisor represents the organisation, and respecting their authority is prudent. While it's beneficial to have independent ideas about our work, it's essential to exercise caution when presenting them prematurely. Prioritising gaining practical experience and aligning with our supervisor's vision during the initial five years is paramount unless ethical or professional concerns exist. While setting personal goals is valuable, our primary focus should be ensuring that our aspirations and actions align with our supervisor's and with the broader organisational objectives.

In a professional setting, it is crucial to embody qualities such as diligence, sincerity, and compliance. Demonstrating a belief in the mission and goals of your organisation is paramount. Bosses greatly value an eager, committed, and respectful approach. It's important to acknowledge that your boss carries specific obligations and seeks to fulfill them most efficiently. When they assess your performance or check you for your inefficiencies, it's not for personal satisfaction but to ensure that tasks are carried out with steadfast commitment and within designated timeframes. It's essential to contemplate how you can further enrich the organisation with your contributions.

It's crucial to recognise that during the early years of your career, your boss is likely to possess more experience and knowledge when it comes to making company policies. This doesn't mean that you are being positioned as a subordinate to suffocate your potential; instead, it reflects the fact that you were chosen by the company to be guided by your boss. Your primary goal should be to align your professional objectives with those of your boss and the organisation. While it's acceptable to provide input occasionally, it's important to remember that your role is to offer guidance, not impose your opinions on others. In the initial stages, listening more and speaking less is crucial, allowing you to comprehend the company's culture and expectations. This will enable you to effectively align your goals with the organisation's while benefiting from your boss's mentorship.

In the workplace, it's common for emotions to influence our behaviour, especially when it comes to interacting with our superiors. It's easy to think that we know better than our bosses and feel compelled to offer unsolicited advice. However, allowing emotions and personal judgments to cloud our actions can have negative consequences. It's important to practice patience and refrain from forming premature opinions. Instead, focus on following instructions and gaining sufficient experience before voicing your thoughts.

Being analytical is important, but it's equally crucial to exercise restraint and wait for the right moment to present your ideas.

Keep a record of your analytical thoughts and revisit them later. If you still believe in your ideas strongly, respectfully approach your boss and present them. Be prepared to step back after presenting your case, and consider preparing a well-organised presentation to articulate your points effectively. This approach increases the chances of your ideas being considered and accepted.

It's essential not to be overly eager for immediate validation from your boss. Learn to elegantly make your case and gracefully step back, regardless of the outcome. Remember, if your advice is not accepted, it doesn't diminish its value. In the long run, your boss will appreciate and trust your input. Good advice, when presented respectfully, is rarely disregarded and often finds its way to being accepted.

Taking Responsibility...Accepting Faults

In Air Force, in air battle practice sessions, we adopt a meticulous approach of analysing the outcomes. Instead of fixating on whether we emerged victorious or suffered a defeat, we meticulously dissect each step of the battle. It is essential to recognise that mistakes are inevitable in every engagement, as each scenario presents its unique complexities. We focus on identifying fundamental and repetitive mistakes to derive meaningful insights and prevent recurring errors. The emphasis on scrutinising individual steps is rooted in the realisation that the final result may not necessarily reflect our capabilities but rather a consequence of the enemy's errors or even a stroke of luck. By breaking down the situation into incremental components, we understand the underlying dynamics better. Likewise, it's imperative to acknowledge that growth can only occur when one is willing to accept their imperfections. Embracing failure in a practice mission and using it as a platform for learning from mistakes is pivotal. The lessons gleaned from these practice missions serve as invaluable tools for navigating real-life combat scenarios.

We all make mistakes from time to time when completing tasks. Throughout my experiences, I have encountered individuals who tend to be quite obstinate. Even if they realise their mistakes, they persist in making excuses rather than acknowledging mistakes. It's crucial to understand the importance of recognising and accepting mistakes. One of the most significant advantages of recognising and accepting errors is that it promptly ends the argument or discussion. Simply apologise, say sorry, and move on; it's not a big deal. On a lighter note, this approach of admitting mistakes can also be applied in your interactions with your spouse. In the case of disagreement with your spouse, accept the mistake even if your spouse is at fault, say sorry and be happy. (Ha..ha..ha).

Accepting and acknowledging one's own mistakes is a fundamental indicator of an exceptional professional mindset. It demonstrates not only a willingness to learn but also the strength of character and courage to admit when things have gone awry. Willingness to accept mistakes as a natural part of learning is critical to personal and professional growth. As a leader, I greatly value and respect individuals who can confidently confront their mistakes. Doing so not only fosters an environment of continuous learning and improvement but it also allows for a humble and grounded approach to personal and professional development.

When you willingly accept accountability for both your positive and negative actions, you gain valuable insights that contribute to your personal growth while also positively influencing those around you. Your behaviour should be a source of inspiration for your peers, motivating them to strive for self-improvement.

Being an Achiever and Being Successful

The concept of being an achiever and being successful encompasses a nuanced distinction. Each individual may perceive success in a unique way, and it's crucial to understand that achieving promotions and a salary increase is not the sole indicator of success. This is often categorised as an achiever, as it revolves around meeting specific goals and targets within a short time frame. Conversely, attaining success is akin to participating in a long-distance race, wherein the focus lies on sustained effort, perseverance, and dedication despite the absence of immediate gratification. It is about consistently treading the chosen path with unwavering commitment, even if the visible results are scarce in the short term. True success extends beyond personal achievements in making a tangible difference in the world, enriching it with one's labour, values, and contributions. It is imperative to wholeheartedly contribute to the betterment of society in any way possible, regardless of the scale of the impact.

Striving for success that leaves a lasting impact is crucial to being remembered for your work. It is important to set long-term goals that not only benefit the individual but also contribute to the growth and success of the organisation. **Regardless of the position one holds, eventually, everyone will retire one day from work**. To be genuinely remembered, it's not enough for achievements to be self-centered or personally goal-oriented. Instead, a legacy is created when success positively impacts the lives of many and adds value to the organisation, society, or humanity as a whole. When your achievements bring about positive change and benefit others, people will remember the impact you made long after you've moved on.

Learning Aptitude

Even though an individual may have established themselves in their profession, it is essential to embrace a mindset of learning and growth continually. Just as Microsoft has realised the importance of regularly upgrading its software, we must strive for continuous improvement. **Learning is an enduring journey that involves unlearning outdated practices and assimilating new knowledge.** It is crucial to be observant and receptive to novel ideas to keep pace with the latest technologies and trends. Remaining enthusiastic about grasping fresh concepts, whether from mentors during challenging periods or from colleagues, is essential. The younger generation's adept use of technology for swift problem-solving offers valuable lessons from their innovative approaches. Since technologies and ideologies evolve annually, staying informed and adapting to these changes is vital. Work cultures and philosophies also undergo transformation every eight to ten years, necessitating flexibility and an open-minded approach.

Creating the habit of daily reading can significantly impact your life in numerous ways. Engaging in the act of reading not only provides an enjoyable pastime but also serves as a valuable practice for personal growth. When you delve into new concepts and ideas through reading, you stimulate your mind, fostering the generation of fresh thoughts and promoting a broader perspective on the world around you.

Incorporating reading into your daily routine is an effective means of developing a higher level of learning aptitude. Whether you are engaging with a captivating novel, a thought-provoking non-fiction book, or even the menu card at a restaurant, every opportunity presents a potential learning experience. Being fully present in every aspect of life, from a dinner date to a routine car service, enables the cultivation of an observant mindset.

During a dinner date, take the opportunity to absorb the ambience of the surroundings and note the intricacies of food presentation. Conversation with the chef about the dish served can unveil insightful details about its creation and ingredients. Furthermore, when servicing your car, seize the chance to converse with the mechanic, as they may impart valuable insights and tips.

Expanding your knowledge base is a continuous journey, and in this pursuit, subjects such as geopolitics, geo-economics, and new technologies hold particular significance. By delving into the literature on geopolitics, you gain a deeper understanding of global dynamics, which in turn aids in comprehending the interconnectedness of geo-economics. This enhanced awareness provides valuable insights into how and why the world operates in a particular manner.

Embracing a regular reading habit expands your mind's horizons, fostering continuous personal growth and intellectual enrichment.

Sometimes Silence Works

In life, there are moments when you may feel like there's no way out and that nobody is on your side. No one is willing to hear you out or empathise with your situation. Even when everything seems to be going wrong, it's important to remember that tough times are a natural part of the human experience. Life is a mix of highs and lows, and it's perfectly alright to take a moment to step back and 'STAY SILENT' for some time. Please take a deep breath, allow yourself to pause for a short while or even a few days, and let things settle at their own pace.

For instance, if you find yourself submerged in water, rather than panicking and struggling, staying silent can help you regain your composure. By staying calm and gently pushing the water downward with your hands, you can use the water's natural buoyancy to help bring you back to the surface. Just like in this example, taking a moment to stay silent and gather your thoughts can yield better results than anxious action.

The most empowering approach is to step back and evaluate your situation after taking a break. It's crucial to examine your challenges from a fresh perspective. For instance, if you're struggling to meet deadlines and feeling pressure from your boss, instead of blaming your boss, try to identify areas where you may be inefficiently using your time. It could be that you need more focused time to complete your tasks. Take time to assess whether you're spending time on unnecessary activities or falling into a pattern of procrastination. Instead of pointing fingers at external factors, it's vital to look inward during these challenging times. Therefore, at times, opting for silence and maintaining stoic demeanour helps. Stoic demeanour allows you hiding your feelings and absorbing things happening around you.

It is vital to take small, deliberate steps to address your situation. Consider reducing your commitments and directing your attention and energies towards resolving the issue at hand. You must recognise that you can only effectively manage one task at a time. You can make better progress by letting go of a few responsibilities and concentrating on the most critical ones.

For instance, if a student is struggling in a particular subject, impacting their overall academic performance, it's crucial to prioritise that weak subject. The student may need to allocate extra time to this subject, even if it means sacrificing personal time or cutting down on the time spent on other subjects.

When faced with multiple problems, it's important to address them individually based on their priority. This approach mirrors the tactics used in aerial combat where, when confronted with several adversaries, the key is to identify the most pressing threat and deal with it first. It's crucial to assess the situation, and if necessary, create an opportunity by stepping back before launching a strategic offensive. If you allow yourself to become overwhelmed, it becomes challenging to regain your footing and effectively engage the challenges at hand. Success in these scenarios hinges on maintaining composure, observing the situation in silence, and launching a vigorous and calculated response.

As a person in a senior position within a company, it's common to face challenges when your viewpoints diverge from those of your top boss. These differences could arise from conflicting ideologies, personal preferences, or individual agendas. In such instances, it is often beneficial to refrain from immediately expressing your dissent. Instead, it's advisable to wait for the right opportunity to address the issue patiently. However, do not hesitate to speak up if you encounter something illegal or unethical or if it disrupts your peace of mind. If you feel compelled to address the situation and create clarity, consider requesting a meeting or looking for an appropriate opportunity to discuss things calmly and respectfully. It's important to acknowledge that ideological clashes among top-level executives are natural and cannot be entirely eradicated. Nevertheless, these conflicts can be mitigated through open and constructive dialogue.

Your personal life is your personal life

In times of crisis or confusion, it's natural to seek a support system. Some individuals tend to openly share their problems with colleagues, hoping to receive empathy and solutions. However, it's essential to remember that our colleagues are not trained professionals in psychology or life coaching, and they are likely have their own challenges to contend with. It's advisable not to rely too heavily on their advice. Instead, it's wise to observe how others handle their own lives. **Over-sharing personal details with colleagues can pose risks, so it's essential to establish and maintain healthy boundaries**

when it comes to discussing personal matters. If you feel the need to talk about personal issues, it's better to speak in general terms. There is a distinct possibility that some colleagues might take advantage of your situation if they are privy to too much information about your personal life.

There are a few important considerations to take into account. Firstly, it's noteworthy that keeping your weaknesses concealed from others can prevent them from exploiting you. While having a support system for seeking advice and assistance during challenging times is essential, it's advisable to seek this outside of your professional environment. It is essential to ensure that individual's values and interests are aligned with you and not at conflicts. Those with conflicting interests may not be able to provide impartial advice. For example, your closest competitor in profession can never advice you appropriately when you are seeking advice on professional matters. Therefore, the most reliable sources of guidance and support often come from your family, childhood friends, or close relatives. Sharing positive and negative experiences with your family is crucial rather than airing them in public. It's essential to keep personal matters private.

Understanding the need to develop the depth and insight to independently analyse and resolve personal challenges is crucial for personal growth. This ability is honed when we lead our lives consciously rather than merely going through the motions. While seeking support from others is essential, it's equally vital to cultivate the maturity and self-reliance necessary to navigate and conquer one's obstacles.

Avoid Conflict at Work

Conflict is an inevitable aspect of the human experience, manifesting in various forms within the workplace. Disagreements may arise between individuals of different hierarchical levels, among peers, or even with superiors. These conflicts can stem from disparities in interests or viewpoints related to professional matters. Furthermore, disagreements may emerge from seemingly inconsequential topics such as movie preferences, allegiance to political parties, or broader societal issues. Notably, discussing political matters and religious beliefs within the armed forces is deliberately avoided as part of our organisational ethos and value system.

In our daily interactions with others, conflicts can often arise as a result of our varying needs, desires, and fears. Each individual, with their unique aspirations and goals, contributes to the fabric of our workplace. It is important to acknowledge and respect the ambitions of others, just as we value our own. Conflict can manifest in various settings such as within families, friendships, and the workplace. Developing the skills to effectively resolve or mitigate conflicts in the workplace is immensely important.

Understanding the intricacies of human psychology and behaviour can be instrumental in reducing conflicts and fostering a more productive environment. Sometimes, approaching situations gently and letting go of specific issues can resolve many disputes. Additionally, it is vital to identify individuals who tend to create workplace disruption and avoid becoming embroiled in their attempts to distract from organisational goals and create unnecessary problems. There is no need to attempt to resolve all the issues at the workplace. Keeping a safe distance or staying silent for some time may resolve specific petty problems.

In the workplace, it is essential to remember that the dynamics of relationships are constantly evolving. We should strive to maintain a balanced approach, neither forming permanent friendships nor holding on to grudges. Navigating workplace interactions is akin to practicing diplomacy, where sometimes, gracefully letting go of a situation can be just as effective as addressing it head-on. **Diplomatic dealing is an art**. It's important to recognise when to tackle challenges directly, when to embrace friendship, and when to engage in negotiation. Negotiation is pivotal in resolving conflicts, allowing us to navigate obstacles thoughtfully and deliberately.

Similar to the strategy employed in aerial combat, engaging in direct confrontation is not always necessary. We don't engage in direct combat all the time. We may choose to approach the enemy from different angles, step back to fight another day, or directly confront the enemy from front when required. It's important to adapt our tactics to the situation and keep our objectives in mind. While a certain degree of conflict in the professional environment can be constructive, swift and effective, conflict resolution is paramount. **Therefore, it's important to choose wisely when to engage, when to step back, and when to ignore.**

When you encounter conflicts with colleagues or peers, it's crucial to start with a self-reflective approach. This involves refraining from immediate confrontation and allowing emotions to settle. By stepping back and giving yourself and others some space, you can gain a clearer, more objective view of the situation. Confrontation should only be considered as a last resort.

Dealing with conflict with your boss can be even more challenging. In this scenario, taking the time to step back and assess the situation is essential. Understanding and comparing your boss's perspective with your own can provide valuable insights. If you find your boss's perspective more reasonable, consider adjusting your approach or waiting for the right opportunity to address the issue diplomatically.

It's crucial not to overwhelm your boss with all of your concerns at once. Taking a step-by-step approach and addressing issues gradually can be more effective. If all attempts to resolve the conflict fail, it may be necessary to have a clear and constructive discussion. While this conversation might carry potential risks, such as the possibility of termination or the need to consider resignation, it's essential to prioritise your well-being when dealing with a toxic work environment. However, it's necessary to make this decision thoughtfully.

As mentioned earlier, some conflict in the workplace can be normal, but if it starts to significantly impact your peace of mind, it's crucial to address it promptly. Whether through direct or indirect means, addressing the conflict in a timely manner can help prevent the situation from escalating and maintain a healthy work environment.

Stay Emotionally Wise

I have a deeply emotional nature and tend to form strong connections with individuals who demonstrate sincerity and integrity. I place great trust in people, often caring for their feelings and well-being. However, I am wary of the possibility of this trust being taken for granted, as I have experienced instances where my initial assessment of individuals turned out to be inaccurate. Therefore, I have learnt to refrain from forming hasty opinions about people upon first interaction. Instead, I believe in taking the time to assess their character and potential honestly.

In my experience, friendships are often based on mutual interests and are not always enduring. While finding a reliable friend in a professional setting is invaluable, I have observed that workplace friendships are frequently short-lived and rooted in shared objectives. Generally, I have placed my trust in hardworking and sincere individuals, but there are no absolute guarantees. Sometimes, people show hard work and sincerity to gain proximity and for inherent interests. My encounters with problems at work have often been linked to interactions with self-centered and irresponsible individuals. In such instances, I have not hesitated to take a firm stance, especially with non-performers and those driven by personal gain. However, not everyone possesses the same capabilities, and it is essential to recognise and respect individuals' diverse needs and desires.

While I advocate for understanding and accommodating individuals' varying needs, professional competence should not be compromised. A balanced approach is necessary; being overly lenient with underperformers can be de-motivating for those who consistently excel. I have learnt to appreciate the varied capabilities of team members and strive to harness each individual's potential effectively.

Our minds operate on two distinct levels, rational and emotional, effectively functioning as two separate entities within the same brain. These two aspects must work in harmony, as they can complement or lead to dominating the other. The Intelligence Quotient (IQ) measures the rational mind's capacity, while the Emotional Quotient (EQ) gauges the emotional mind's capabilities. I've come to realise in my later years that EQ is equally, if not more, significant than IQ, mainly when dealing with challenging, unreasonable, or unpredictable personalities. In such situations, a high EQ often trumps a high IQ.

Developing emotional intelligence is a crucial aspect of personal growth and effective leadership. It involves the ability to recognise, understand, and manage one's emotions while also being attuned to the feelings of others. **Emotional intelligence enables individuals to navigate social complexities, make sound decisions, and adapt to various situations.**

One key aspect of emotional intelligence is the empowering capacity to control one's emotions and not allow external influences to manipulate them. This involves maintaining composure in challenging situations and not letting emotions cloud judgment. It also entails the empowering ability to handle conflicts without becoming emotionally drained, allowing individuals to navigate interpersonal challenges with resilience and grace, and ultimately, to be in control of their emotional responses.

Furthermore, emotional intelligence involves the adept use of communication skills. Utilising soft and persuasive language can often be more effective than resorting to forceful or direct communication, mainly when dealing with individuals who may not respond well to assertiveness. Empathy and understanding play a crucial role in effectively communicating with others, especially those who may be uncooperative or resistant to strict directives.

Recognising that not everyone responds well to rigid approaches and considering the needs and interests of others is essential. Fostering empathy and understanding for those who may be difficult to work with can help mitigate potential conflicts and build more harmonious relationships. By approaching challenging situations with tact and emotional intelligence, individuals cannot only navigate complexities but also foster positive outcomes, bringing a sense of hope and optimism to the table.

Emotional intelligence is a crucial skill that we all need to develop in order to navigate the complexities of human interactions. It is imperative that we remain empathetic and emotionally aware, particularly when engaging with individuals who demonstrate sincerity and hard work. Respecting and valuing the emotions of honest, passionate, and hardworking individuals is essential, as these qualities are often rare.

In addition to considering individual emotions, it's crucial to recognise and respect cultural differences, such as those related to caste, creed, religion, and gender. Sensitivity to these variations is not just important, it's necessary. Adapting to these differences is a key step in fostering genuine connections and understanding.

Emotional intelligence encompasses the ability to comprehend and navigate one's own emotions while also being attuned to the feelings of others. This multifaceted skill cannot be simply defined in a few words, as it involves a deep understanding of human emotions.

In my personal experience, I have encountered challenges when dealing with individuals who possess intricate personalities. As I continue to grow, I have learnt that developing emotional intelligence is not a one-time task but a continuous journey. I want to share some strategies for effectively engaging with complex individuals, emphasising the ongoing commitment required. Here are some suggestions for handling such situations: -

- It is essential to choose your battles wisely in the workplace, mainly when dealing with challenging or uncooperative individuals. Trying to win every conflict may create unnecessary tension and hinder overall productivity.
- Don't invest too much energy in engaging with individuals behaving foolishly or uncooperatively. However, it's also important not to completely dismiss them or their perspectives.
- When providing feedback to someone, it's essential to exercise caution and choose words that convey your message with respect and consideration rather than resorting to directly calling them foolish.
- When addressing an underperformer, it's essential to approach the situation with empathy and understanding. Begin by having a one-on-one conversation with them to express your concerns and let them know you value their contributions to the team. Assure you are there to support them and are committed to helping them succeed. During this initial conversation, your main objective should be to

make them feel comfortable and at ease so that you can work together to address the performance issues.

- When dealing with difficult individuals, it's important to try to understand their perspective and find ways to redirect their efforts more productively. If you find it challenging to communicate with them, it's best to remain patient and suggest that they come back later. Reacting with anger should always be the last option after exhausting all other possibilities.

- It's essential to remember that it's often difficult to influence or change the mindset of specific complex individuals. These people are typically very set in their ways and resistant to change. It's wise to be selective about the time and energy you invest in trying to influence them, and it may be best to keep a polite distance while maintaining a relationship based on necessity.

- It's important to stay calm and composed when interacting with an unreasonable person. Avoid the temptation to respond in anger, as doing so will only escalate the situation and give the other person more power. Instead, it's the best to distance yourself from such individuals and focus on maintaining peace of mind.

- When dealing with complex individuals, consider making an effort to recognise some positive attributes in them and leverage those qualities until you can make peace with them.

- It's important to understand that in certain circumstances, it can be more advantageous to disengage from an unreasonable individual and refocus your efforts on more meaningful activities. This strategy enables you to maintain control over your actions and energy instead of fruitlessly attempting to change the behaviour of someone who may not act rationally. When dealing with difficult or unreasonable individuals, it's wise to exercise patience. Some people may attempt to draw you into their negative behaviour, similar to how a pig enjoys mud wrestling. It's crucial not to allow them to take over your emotions. If someone is trying to provoke you, the best course of action is to avoid, ignore, and change the subject, allowing you to address the situation calmly later. Don't allow people to hijack your emotions.

- It's essential to avoid confrontations with underperforming or troublesome individuals whenever possible. When faced with such situations, these individuals may seek to form alliances against you and damage your reputation. Moreover, individuals like these often have a little to lose and may resort to using any means available, whether legal or not, to pull you down.

- Strive to maintain fairness and openness in all your interactions and actions. It's essential not only to be correct but also to show that you are transparent and exemplary in your actions and decisions. This approach will go a long way in minimising conflicts that can be avoided. **Your team looks up to a fair, transparent leader who can call a spade a spade**. Subordinates will have greater respect for an upright and decisive leader, no matter their relationship with the leader.

- When a leader demonstrates fair and impartial behaviour, it helps to reduce conflicts and fosters an environment where people view them as trustworthy and non-manipulative.

- Daniel Goleman, renowned for his best-selling book 'Emotional Intelligence,' defines emotional intelligence (EQ) as a vital tool for personal and professional development. According to Goleman, EQ enhances our ability to understand and manage ourselves, empathise with others, navigate social complexities, and handle relationships effectively. These elements of EQ serve as a driving force, encouraging and propelling us to achieve greater success and fulfillment in all aspects of our lives.

One-Third of Life at Workplace

While listening to a conversation featuring the Indian spiritual guru Sadhguru, I profoundly realised how much time we spend at work. Consider calculating working hours out of the 24 hours a day, we typically allocate around eight hours for sleep, three to four hours for daily chores, and another two hours for commuting to and from work. This leaves us with roughly eight to ten hours to dedicate to our work responsibilities. It's eye-opening to recognise that we devote more than one third of our waking hours to our jobs.

Given the significant portion of our lives that we spend at work, it becomes crucial to ensure that we are able to make the most of this time. Balancing our energy and mental well-being in the workplace is essential for our overall fulfillment and productivity. Each one of us has the responsibility to create a positive and enriching work environment.

To achieve this, we should proactively work towards eliminating any unnecessary physical or mental clutter before we even enter the workplace. We must view our work environment as a space that deserves the same level of attention and care as we can look forward to our personal and leisure time. By fostering a positive and enjoyable atmosphere at work, we can significantly enhance our overall work experience.

Neglecting the care and maintenance of our workplace can affect our productivity and well-being. Creating a harmonious and supportive work environment benefits us individually and contributes to a healthier and more productive workplace culture overall.

I've noticed some individuals come to work after attending late-night parties or long weekends; even some are used to being glued to television until late at night. As a result, they often appear to be sleep-deprived and may even be experiencing hangovers from the previous night or weekend festivities. Due to a lack of adequate sleep and rest, they often struggle with feeling drowsy and fatigued throughout the day, which inevitably impacts their productivity at work. This type of behaviour is not considered professional as it can lead to irritability and an inability to perform at one's best due to the body and mind not being in an optimal state. We must rethink our approach and strive to create a work environment that promotes energy, enthusiasm, and happiness. By cultivating happiness in the workplace, we can significantly enhance one-third of our lives, typically spent at work. It's essential to actively choose happiness rather than passively waiting for it to occur.

If you're finding that your work life is not going well, it's essential to recognise that the reasons behind this may go beyond your actions. Many individuals face challenges related to toxic work environments, difficult colleagues, and problematic or indecisive bosses. Toxic colleagues and bosses can behave like politicians in the workplace, with their agenda being to spread negativity and derive satisfaction from undermining others. Generally, these individuals are unprofessional and may feel threatened by your professional competence. Suppose you're struggling to cope with the stress and negative atmosphere at your workplace due to such colleagues or bosses. In that case, it's essential to consider finding a new workplace or getting out of the negative environment by any means. Since work life takes up a significant amount of our life, prioritising our well-being is crucial.

It's normal to experience challenges that make it hard to find happiness for a significant portion of your life, especially when these challenges relate to your boss, colleagues, or work environment. Quitting your job immediately might not be feasible due to various reasons. In such situations, it's best to take some time to gather your thoughts, remain silent for a few days, and then constructively communicate your concerns with your colleagues or boss once things have settled.

Take the time to reflect on your situation, reassess your approach, and let go of things that may impact your well-being. Prioritise important tasks, consider taking a break, and engage in physical activities such as walking, yoga, or going to the gym. By following these steps, you will gradually notice improvements in your situation. It's crucial to actively design this part of your life to be fulfilling and joyful rather than relying on external factors for your happiness.

If we make one-third of our life comfortable and beautiful, there will be only a few hours left to manage, most of which will be spent in bed sleeping. Therefore, it's essential to prioritise our personal lives and social activities as much as our work. Remember that **work enables us to enjoy other aspects of life, so strive to maintain happiness and positivity in the workplace**.

Professional Growth

Your professional abilities don't solely determine advancements in your career. Numerous factors contribute to your professional growth. It's crucial to focus on holistic development within your job role. As time progresses, your professional skills are just one aspect of your overall progress. I don't deny the importance of professional skills. They remain just as crucial as they were at the start of your career. However, it's essential to complement your professional skills with other qualities and soft skills. It's akin to preparing a delicious dish is one aspect while presenting it appealingly another. While garnishing the dish might not alter its taste, it enhances its visual appeal. Some beneficial characteristics to cultivate within ourselves include kindness, honesty, empathy, resilience, adaptability, patience, and perseverance. These traits can help us navigate life's challenges and build solid and meaningful relationships with others. The following characteristics one must try to develop in oneself: -

- Facing challenges is a universal experience, and the very essence of a challenge is to put you in a state of uncertainty, which can impede your ability to make decisions. Once you acquire the skill to methodically and thoroughly analyse challenges, you can resolve them effectively. The quality of decisions you make in times of crisis or when under pressure defines your character. Anyone can assume the role of a leader or a commander in ordinary circumstances, but it is during crises that an individual's true character is laid bare. Cultivating analytical and decision-making capabilities is crucial for steering through crises successfully. Remember that your subordinates rely on you for guidance through your choices. I've observed leaders who shy away from challenging situations, deliberate excessively, or refrain from making decisions, choosing instead to wait for issues to resolve themselves. I have learnt, "**Not making a decision is also a decision, but a poor one**".

- Completing a task is more than just finishing it—it's about striving for excellence. Set yourself apart by meticulously examining every detail and devising contingency plans or alternative solutions. Even when assigned a seemingly minor task, dedicate your focus to scrutinising all aspects and striving to produce top-notch outcomes. Always make it a habit to allocate an extra five to ten minutes to review and refine your work before presenting it.

- Effective communication is a crucial skill that can elevate your expertise in any field. Even if you possess extensive knowledge, articulating your thoughts clearly, whether orally or in writing, is essential for achieving the desired impact. The ability to convey your ideas with clarity and logic is incredibly compelling. When you can influence others with your words, you naturally garner respect. Look at how politicians and business leaders use concise yet persuasive language to capture the public's imagination. Consider, for instance, the impact of Steve Jobs' iconic 2005 Stanford commencement address. When you can express yourself effectively, you possess the power to resonate deeply with anyone. Strong communication skills have the potential to untangle even the most intricate problems. Cultivating the ability to sway others with your words is a mighty endeavour. Remarkably, over 50% of issues can be resolved through effective communication. When I speak of communication skills, I also refer to the valuable trait of listening attentively. You can effortlessly forge connections with those around you by honing your ability to articulate your ideas expressively and truly hear others.

- Some individuals possess an innate talent for swiftly comprehending concepts simply by visualising them. This unique ability can be honed by deconstructing complex ideas into smaller, more digestible components. Rather than perceiving concepts as a whole, the process begins by dissecting them into parts and establishing connections with familiar knowledge. For instance, breaking down a lengthy ten-digit phone number into manageable groups of two or three digits can facilitate memorisation. **Enhancing one's capacity for rapid information absorption can significantly improve analytical skills and vice versa**.

- To earn the appreciation of any boss, it's essential to demonstrate a strong sense of ownership and initiative within the organisation. This involves going beyond the responsibilities of your current role and proactively considering the organisation's future needs. Developing the ability to think and act independently for the benefit of the organisation is crucial. This can be achieved through engaging in activities such as conducting in-depth research, writing insightful papers, creating analytical reports, and delivering impactful presentations.

- Impressing your boss involves going above and beyond what is expected of you. Taking the initiative, differentiating yourself from your peers, and willingly taking on challenging projects to demonstrate your capabilities are critical components of earning the appreciation of any boss.

- It is to be understood that resources are always finite in any organisation. That's precisely why humans are such a crucial part of any workforce, as they can adapt to less-than-ideal conditions and make the most of what's available. Else, robots would have been employed everywhere in place of humans. No work environment is perfect. Perfection at the workplace is a myth. Your primary goal should be to truly understand the unique demands of your role and then deploy the resources at your disposal in the most effective way possible to achieve maximum productivity. You can achieve your organisational goals by identifying and focusing on the most critical tasks, even with constraints.

Professionals are typically focused on one direction, but influential leaders need to be able to manage multiple tasks simultaneously. To be an influential leader, it's essential to handle multiple responsibilities at once, overseeing various activities and coordinating with others to achieve objectives. Inter-department friction is common, but efforts should be made to coordinate tasks and minimise conflicts. Use all tactics to coordinate things, be it ignore, avoid, diplomacy, bend, retreat, or straight talk, but resolve the issues. Positive workplace relationships can significantly enhance productivity.

It's common for different departments to have friction, so it's crucial to coordinate tasks and reduce conflicts. Employ a range of tactics, such as ignoring minor issues, using diplomatic approaches, adapting to different situations, or having straightforward conversations to address and resolve any conflicts that may arise. Building positive relationships in the workplace can lead to increased productivity and overall success.

Leadership

Leadership skills are essential not only for those in top positions but also for individuals in lower positions within an organisation. At times, a peon or a clerk can exhibit exceptional leadership skills that surpass those of senior managers. Effective leadership goes beyond wielding authority—it involves taking on responsibility for one's role, demonstrating integrity towards the organisation, and being prepared to fulfill the duties assigned by the organisation. It encompasses the honest and sincere management of the organisation's resources, serving as an exemplary role model, and taking charge during times of crisis. Genuine leadership is about staying true to oneself while inspiring and guiding others, ultimately contributing to the collective betterment of all involved.

To exemplify my point, consider the often overlooked yet pivotal role played by the staff who that diligently manages our offices, eagerly serve tea or coffee when we're exhausted, and take on numerous seemingly minor tasks. Despite being the least-paid employee, this individual shoulders the significant responsibility of simplifying and managing the lives of those striving to attain the organisation's objectives. While this person's contribution doesn't directly impact the organisation's growth, their unwavering dedication is a powerful force multiplier. Presenting a well-made cup of coffee after a draining meeting revitalises us, leading to increased work efficiency as we pursue the organisation's goals. Moreover, maintaining a clean and tidy workplace daily imparts unseen energy and positivity that propels our efforts. By executing their responsibilities with utmost sincerity and hard work, these individuals amplify the overall happiness within the office and exemplify leadership qualities within their roles. It's crucial not to underestimate the significance of these small yet impactful contributions. Such individuals often carry out their duties without supervision, exemplifying an unwavering commitment to the organisation. They are the first ones to arrive and the last to leave, distinctly showcasing their dedication to their responsibilities.

In the military, the individual responsible for preparing meals for troops plays a pivotal role in accomplishing mission objectives. In this seemingly small but vital position, they demonstrate exemplary leadership qualities such as accountability, diligence, dedication, adept time management, and many other admirable traits.

Regardless of the size of the role, it is crucial to showcase leadership skills, as they play a significant role in personal growth and in contributing to the accomplishment of organisational goals. Hence, it is imperative to prioritise the development of leadership qualities right from the onset of one's career.

Leadership traits are not dependent on one's position within an organisation. Learning leadership tools early in one's career is essential for making a significant impact. Your early leadership development serves as evidence of one's potential and the value one brings to the organisation.

Balancing and managing individuals' diverse personalities and behaviours in a work environment can be challenging. It is essential to prioritise our well-being and the well-being of our colleagues. Creating a comfortable and harmonious work environment does not necessarily mean that everyone must always be in a state of perpetual happiness, as this would be an unrealistic and unattainable goal. Rather, it requires us to provide support to some, offer constructive feedback to others, and handle certain situations with tact and diplomacy.

A key aspect of this balancing act is the need to prioritise the organisation's goals and objectives while treating everyone with love, care, firmness, respect, and transparency. Our actions reflect our dedication, sincerity, ethical conduct, dignity, and integrity, showcasing that we are resolute, decisive, optimistic, innovative, and forward-thinking. Demonstrating these qualities is essential for earning the trust and support of our colleagues.

Moreover, understanding human psychology is crucial for effective management. This understanding allows us to navigate the intricacies of human behaviour and motivations, enabling us to lead and support our teams more informed and empathetically.

To effectively lead a team, it is essential to invest time and effort in understanding each team member's unique strengths and weaknesses. A leader can foster a more cohesive and productive team dynamic by recognising and leveraging individual strengths rather than simply focusing on weaknesses. Delegating tasks and responsibilities is a crucial aspect of leadership, as it allows a leader to empower team members while still maintaining overall accountability. Some leaders may struggle with relinquishing control and prefer to oversee every task personally, but effective delegation is vital for the team's and its members' growth. Furthermore, cultivating leadership qualities that enable a smooth transition from team member to leader is critical in facilitating a positive and effective work environment.

Understanding Human Psychology

Understanding human psychology is a significant factor that can significantly enhance your personality and give you a competitive edge in various aspects of life. While delving into the depths of human psychology is a complex and vast subject that cannot be mastered overnight, it is a skill worth pursuing. Striving to comprehend the needs, motivations, and desires of others can significantly impact our interactions and relationships. When we have insight into the requirements of the people we are dealing with, we are better equipped to tailor our approach and communication effectively, leading to more positive and fruitful outcomes in our interactions.

It's essential to bear in mind that everyone aspires to excel in their endeavours. We all seek advancement, whether in terms of career progression, social standing, or financial gain. Each of us adopts unique approaches to handling situations. Some individuals tackle challenges head-on with unwavering integrity, diligence, and hard work. Others prefer employing diplomatic and tactful strategies. Some rely solely on personal connections (PR) to accomplish their objectives through influence and flattery. It's challenging to unequivocally determine the most effective approach to handling situations as each tactic has advantages and drawbacks. The human mind is incredibly complex, comparable to a supercomputer, capable of generating results through diverse methodologies. Not everyone functions at the same wavelength, and it's essential to recognise and appreciate this diversity.

It is essential to have a balanced blend of different qualities in various circumstances. Maintaining a balance of 50% Professionalism, 30% Diplomacy, and 20% Public Relations is crucial. However, this ratio can be adjusted depending on individual capabilities and specific needs. For example, individuals who may lack professionalism can increase their focus on diplomacy or public relations to navigate complex situations effectively.

I strongly believe in embracing core values such as truthfulness, hard work, and honesty. These qualities are not just fundamental; they are the bedrock of achieving sustained success. It is imperative to prioritise progress without resorting to unethical practices or compromising our colleagues' and subordinates' dreams and ambitions. Upholding these values can inspire and motivate us to be the best versions of ourselves in our professional lives.

Assisting others in achieving their goals can ultimately contribute to our success. When we selflessly support others in reaching their objectives, we foster an environment of collaboration and mutual growth that can elevate everyone involved. It's essential to remember that our time in this world is limited, and we should strive to create a positive and nurturing environment for everyone. This means emphasising genuine connections, empathy, and understanding. Rather than engaging in political games filled with propaganda, distrust, and selfishness. We should focus on building meaningful relationships and uplifting one another. Doing so can create a harmonious and supportive community that benefits all its members.

Workplace Dynamics

Understanding the intricacies of workplace dynamics is essential for successfully navigating professional environments. It's important to recognise the diversity of needs, desires, and aspirations among colleagues and to tailor our interactions and communications accordingly. **When conflicts arise, it's crucial to develop the ability to discern when to address issues and when to let certain matters go**. Rather than focusing on "winning" arguments, the primary goal of discussions should be to gain mutual understanding. This can be achieved by setting aside personal agendas and seeking common ground. It's also important to acknowledge that in the workplace, the landscape of alliances and animosities is constantly shifting based on resolved or unresolved interests and issues. By cultivating a comprehensive understanding of workplace dynamics and exercising diplomacy in our interactions, we can contribute to a positive and harmonious work environment for ourselves and our colleagues.

There is no alternative to hard work. It doesn't matter if you're a genius like Albert Einstein or an average person; you have to carve out your position in the workplace. The only thing you can count on is putting in the effort. It would help if you worked diligently and sincerely. It's essential to learn and refine your skills continually. **Align yourself with your organisation's mission and make its objectives your own**. Building strong relationships will enhance your personality and help you win people over. No one will hand you your position; you must earn it through dedication. While you may not see immediate results, the effort will pay off in the long run. Adopting this approach as part of your personality will yield long-term benefits. Addressing your weaknesses is a continual process; keep working on them to improve daily.

In our journey through life, it's essential always to prioritise our happiness, regardless of the challenges that come our way. Workplaces can sometimes be a breeding ground for conflicts, but it's crucial not to let these conflicts linger and weigh us down. Instead, we should strive to release the negativity and embrace a mindset focused on happiness, especially in the face of adversity. It's essential to recognise that our time in this world is fleeting, and as such, we shouldn't let success or failure define our essence. We should approach success and failure with equanimity, staying calm and resolute as we progress. By focusing on happiness, we can pave the way for positive outcomes to manifest in our lives.

Takeaways from Chapter-1

- It's crucial to prioritise continuous learning, relationship building, and meaningful contributions to your organisation's growth.

- Regardless of your position, embodying leadership qualities from the outset is essential, as these skills hold value at every stage of your professional journey.

- Stress the value of enduring workplace challenges, as they can cultivate resilience and inner strength, which are key qualities for career progression.

- Underline the importance of discovering your IKIGAI, or your reason for being, as it leads to personal fulfillment and professional excellence.

- It's impossible to replicate exceptional individuals; however, we can draw inspiration from their actions.

- Approaching your work sincerely and earnestly opens the door to limitless learning and growth.

- Embrace the advice to speak less and listen more at the start of your career, letting your actions and dedication speak for you.

- There's no substitute for excelling in your core responsibilities. Acknowledging and addressing your weaknesses will pave the way for long-term success.

- Recognising and addressing your weaknesses is essential for achieving long-term success.

- During the initial stages of building your career, strive to elevate yourself to version 2.0 or beyond, focusing on personal development and enhancement.

- Effective communication skills are a source of empowerment, enabling you to connect with others and effectively resolve conflicts.
- It's essential to embrace failures as an inevitable part of life and learn to handle setbacks with grace and resilience.
- A solid belief in your organisation's mission and goals is vital for professional success.
- Acknowledging and learning from mistakes is essential to an exceptional professional mindset.
- Always set ambitious, long-term goals for yourself. Thinking big is essential to achieving great success.
- Learning is a perpetual journey that involves unlearning outdated practices and embracing new knowledge.
- Life is full of ups and downs, and it's completely acceptable to take a moment to step back and remain silent during difficult times.
- When confronted with multiple problems, it's essential to address each one individually and based on its level of priority.
- It's wise to keep your personal life private, sharing it only with a trusted few or saving it for yourself.
- Conflict is an inevitable part of the human experience and can manifest in various forms in the workplace. It's best to avoid, ignore, or diffuse conflicts, but resolving them as soon as possible is crucial.
- In the workplace, diplomatic handling of interactions is an art.
- Developing emotional intelligence is a vital aspect of personal growth and effective leadership. It's important to understand that individuals have diverse needs and desires.

- As we spend a significant portion of our lives in the workplace, it's essential to approach our work with mindfulness and intention.

- Creating a positive and enjoyable atmosphere at work can profoundly impact our overall work experience, leading to greater satisfaction and productivity.

- We have ample time to manage other aspects of our lives when we have a comfortable work-life balance.

- Regardless of the size of our role, leadership skills are essential for personal growth and contributing to achieving organisational goals.

- It's crucial to balance professionalism, diplomacy, and public relations in different situations. Maintaining a blend of 50% professionalism, 30% diplomacy, and 20% public relations can be critical to successfully navigating various professional scenarios.

- In the journey of life, it's essential for us to place a high value on our happiness, even when faced with difficult circumstances.

CHAPTER 2

LET'S CREATE WEALTH

Money Does Not Grow on Trees

Earning money requires effort and hard work; it does not simply appear out of nowhere. It is essential to grasp the fundamental principles of wealth creation and management to build wealth.

Understanding the concept of money involves two key aspects: earning and spending. While both are crucial, the skill of spending money wisely holds greater significance in the journey towards wealth creation. While learning to generate income is essential, knowing how to allocate and spend it judiciously is basic requirement for securing long-term financial stability and accumulating wealth. The definition of wealth is subjective and is contingent upon individual requirements. One can lead a content life with minimal financial resources by curtailing one's needs. Conversely, even a substantial sum of money may prove inadequate if one's needs are extensive.

Money plays a vital role in our lives as it is necessary not just for survival but also for pursuing passions and making meaningful contributions to society. From supporting the arts, fueling innovation, and enabling charitable endeavours to participate in nation-building, wealth is crucial. As responsible citizens, it is essential to strive for financial success to contribute to the advancement of our country. While a few million rupees can cover living expenses, wealth provides the power to establish businesses, construct infrastructure, enhance public facilities, and assist others; ultimately driving progress and positive changes in individual's life and in society.

Utilising our finances involves two primary aspects: expenditure and investment. These elements are closely connected, emphasising the importance of striking a harmonious balance between them. It's crucial to ensure that our spending is directed towards enhancing our overall well-being, prioritising genuine needs over the impulse to keep up with others or flaunt material wealth to show off to our family or friends.

In his best-selling book 'Rich Dad Poor Dad,' Robert T. Kiyosaki delves into the fundamental concepts of assets and liabilities to provide invaluable financial advice. Kiyosaki encourages readers to prioritise spending on assets – things that will increase their power and improve their abilities, instead of acquiring liabilities primarily to impress others. He emphasises that by spending money wisely on necessary items and saving the rest, individuals can build wealth and be free to utilise it for any purpose. This underscores the importance of making informed financial decisions and prioritising acquiring assets over liabilities to pursue long-term financial well-being.

Let's consider your commuting situation as an example. If your workplace is an hour's drive from your home and you're tired of spending two hours every day in traffic, investing in a fuel-efficient and comfortable car might be a good idea. You could also consider hiring a driver to take over the driving responsibilities, allowing you to use your commuting time more productively. In this case, it's worth spending money on a comfortable car and a driver to improve your daily commute. On the other hand, if your office is just a 10-minute drive from home, there's no need for a driver or an expensive car. It would be unnecessary to invest in a luxury car when you'll hardly be using it for a short commute. In fact, consider using public transport or a cab instead of purchasing a car. Some financially savvy individuals opt for second-hand cars, viewing a car simply as a means of transportation. If you're early in your career, it's wise to minimise spending on liabilities like purchasing a car or an expensive bike.

Getting rid of the Mediocre Mentality

I often use the term "Mediocre Mentality" to illustrate a mindset where individuals prioritise spending money on projecting status and upholding a particular image in society rather than utilising it for their betterment. Individuals can be categorised into three classes based on income and spending patterns: lower, middle, and upper. It's important to note that I don't employ these categories to elevate or diminish anyone but rather to gain insight into how individuals earn and allocate their finances. While it's relatively straightforward to differentiate between the lower and upper classes, defining the middle class presents a more complex challenge. Within the middle class, there are additional subcategories, including the lower and upper middle classes.

The lower class faces significant challenges in meeting their daily needs due to unreliable and insufficient monthly earnings. This hinders their ability to afford a comfortable lifestyle and often necessitates assistance in providing their children with primary and higher education. In contrast, the higher class enjoys the ability to afford luxuries and does not face the same level of concern when it comes to meeting their daily needs.

One approach to delineating social classes is to consider the ability of individuals to finance their children's education. Typically, lower-class people can afford primary education for their children but face challenges in funding higher education. Middle-class individuals can often support their children's higher education but may need to make significant financial sacrifices to fulfill their children's aspirations. In some cases, middle-class families may even take out education loans to provide their children with expanded opportunities. Meanwhile, those in the upper class can readily afford to provide their children with high-quality higher education and may even send them abroad for their studies.

So far, I have classified people based solely on their financial situations. Generally, a person's financial status can significantly influence their mindset due to their different needs and aspirations. Ultimately, our belonging to a specific class is determined by our mindset, needs, and aspirations.

A person from the middle class often struggles throughout their lives to prove their status and wealth to their peers, relatives, and friends. They find it challenging to define their needs and desires and frequently attempt to keep up with those in higher social classes by acquiring expensive possessions such as mobile phones, cars, and houses. Even if their monthly salary is 1.5 lakh, they may aspire to own the latest iPhone model, which costs approximately the same as their monthly take-home pay. Rather than increasing their income, middle-class individual often seek to elevate their social status through spending. They may try to emulate the lifestyle of the upper class by purchasing luxury items, such as an expensive watch or mobile phone, or by showing off a high-end car to friends and relatives, even if they have bought these items on credit.

I can share numerous anecdotes of extravagant Indian weddings where middle-class parents spend their hard-earned money as if it were effortlessly earned. It's astonishing to see millions of rupees spent in just one night at a wedding. However, it takes years to accumulate this wealth. These parents don't necessarily wish to spend such a large amount on weddings, but they feel compelled to do so due to social pressure. A significant portion of this money is wasted on unnecessary expenses such as lavish decorations, venue charges, and food. At this age, middle-class parents spend 30 to 50 lakhs of rupees on a single wedding, including jewellery, clothing, food, decorations, and venue bookings. Wedding costs can be reduced by minimising expenditures on large venues, decorations, food, and extravagant attire. If this saved money is given to the newlywed couple, they can begin their married life with a solid financial foundation. They can enhance their quality of life from the beginning of their marriage. There are numerous instances where the bride's parents have taken out loans for their daughters' weddings to meet societal expectations.

An expensive car or a lavish wedding may attract attention in society for a short while. You might show off to your friends and family, but this won't bring lasting satisfaction. Many middle-class people make decisions based on the expectations of others rather than just to fulfill their own needs. However, these expectations are not always reasonable. It's important to remember that "PEOPLE WILL TALK WHATEVER YOU DO". **We should not let others' opinions dictate our choices.** I'm not suggesting becoming rebellious and turning our eyes on society, but rather advocating for making wise and conscious decisions that prioritise our needs and desires over others' opinions. **Mediocrity arises when we constantly seek validation from others and compete in every aspect of life.** It's a mindset where we act solely to please others and seek their approval. If you make purchases to impress others, you may be operating with a mediocre mentality.

Experiencing the joy of receiving uplifting remarks and gratitude for sporting an elegant shirt, well-fitting trousers, fashionable shoes, or owning a luxurious car can be truly exhilarating. Such compliments elevate our spirits and impart a sense of contentment. When we are commended for our physical appearance or priced possessions, it triggers a surge in dopamine levels within our system. Often hailed as the "happy hormone," dopamine is closely linked to overall happiness and gratification sensations.

It's important to remember that there are more sustainable approaches than purchasing items solely to boost dopamine levels. Numerous cost-effective methods exist to increase dopamine levels, and it's worth exploring these alternatives. Some individuals engage in shopping as a means to experience a sense of excitement, alleviate stress, or elevate their dopamine levels. Purchasing expensive, well-known brands gives them a sense of satisfaction, especially when they showcase these items at social events and gatherings. While there's nothing inherently wrong with enjoying nice clothing, **it's essential to maintain a balanced perspective and not allow material possessions to become the sole focus of one's life**.

I want to reiterate the points I made earlier. It's important to shift your focus from simply showcasing your possessions to considering the practical value they hold, and from meeting your ego's desires to meeting your actual needs. Ultimately, it's your hard-earned money, and how you choose to utilise it is entirely up to you. By accumulating wealth responsibly, you can afford the things you truly want at any time. However, misusing your wealth by accumulating unnecessary items can lead to needing more wealth to offset these liabilities. This can create a vicious cycle of materialistic spending, where the more you have, the more you want, and the more you need to work to sustain it. In today's world, it's possible to quickly acquire almost anything, either online or offline, as long as you have the means to afford it. Once you have the necessary resources, you can make substantial purchases, such as a car, within a matter of hours, either in person or online.

Investment and Wealth Creation

When looking to invest and grow your money, it's crucial to consider options that outpace inflation and yield a positive return. Inflation refers to the rise in the cost of goods and services over time, typically measured annually. It's essential to entrust your hard-earned money only to government-recognised individuals or organisations. Beware of being enticed by friends, acquaintances, builders, or private investment firms offering high returns (as much as 25 to 30%), as they often lack credibility. Despite any agreements or assurances they provide, these investments pose an unacceptable level of risk. In the unfortunate event of fraud, even if legal action is pursued and successful, the process can be long-drawn-out and emotionally draining, making it more trouble than it's worth. Following are various ways of investments with their average **expected** rate of returns: -

Investment method	Average rate of return in last 20 years
Banks – FDs	6 to 7 %[ii]
Gold/ Silver	10 to 11%[iii]
Real Estate	9 to 10%[iv]
Govt Bonds, Govt Schemes	8%[v]
Equity Mutual Funds	14 to 16%[vi]
Index Funds/ ETFs (e.g. Nifty 50)	12 to 15%[vii]
Direct in Equity	15 to 20%[viii]

Please note that the rates of return provided in the table above are sourced from the internet (Please see the references) and are based on the historical performance (over the last 10 to 20 years) of these investment methods. It's essential to approach these figures with caution as they may vary, and future returns could differ from past performance. Remember that 20 years is a significant time period, and returns are likely to be more or less same as given in references.

I've learnt the importance of developing the habit of regular investing as early as possible. It's essential to stay invested to build wealth over time, unless you need the money. I have my personal preferences and thought processes regarding various investment methods, all of which I've gained through the experience of making mistakes in multiple investments. *Before continuing, I want to emphasise that I am not providing financial advice or investment tips. My goal is to increase awareness about the investment process and wealth creation. Everyone must conduct thorough research or consult financial experts before making investment decisions.* In brief, I will tell you the pros and cons of all these methods: -

Investment method	Pros	Cons
Banks – FDs	Super safe, Hassle free, Fixed Return	Can't even beat inflation or may be just saving the value of your money
Gold/ Silver	Safe, Physically available asset, Higher returns than FDs, Good results in long term	Liquidity issue if bought in kind, Physical safety issue, Emotional attachment so generally become dead asset
Real Estate	Physically available asset, Higher returns than FDs,	Lots of hassles in buying and selling, Possibility of Legal issues and fraud,

Investment method	Pros	Cons
		Securing it from illegal possessions
Govt Bonds, Govt Schemes	Super safe, Hassle free, Fixed Return, Returns higher than FDs	Money gets blocked for bond period
Mutual Funds	Safe, Fund manager managing your portfolio, Moderate to good returns	Moderate to High Risk, Market dependent, Moderate to heavy exit load
Index Mutual Funds, ETFs (e.g. Nifty 50)	Safer than Mutual Funds, Investment in basket of stocks therefore risk averaging, Good returns in long run, relatively safer as compared to direct stocks, Generally beat more than 50 % mutual funds	Moderate to High Risk, Market dependent
Direct in Equity	Good returns expected, Demands knowledge, Time consuming and monitoring	Market dependent, **Highly volatile**, **May destroy investment**

Stock Market Volatility

Understanding the stock market is essential before diving into direct stock investment. **The stock market is complex and unpredictable, making it a daunting choice for many individuals.** To enter the stock market, one must grasp its dynamics and the many factors that drive its fluctuations. Engaging with the stock market demands comprehensive research and analysis of various stocks, which can be challenging for those without specialised knowledge in finance.

It's a common pitfall for individuals to venture into the stock market without conducting thorough research. They often lean on recommendations from friends, family, or information found on the internet and social media. Unfortunately, this approach can lead to losses due to the lack of comprehensive and sometimes inaccurate knowledge. It's essential to recognise that not everyone is an expert in the stock market, as we all come from diverse professional backgrounds, and stock market investing is a specialised field.

Working professionals must focus on their specific fields and avoid getting caught up in the complexities of direct stock market investment. Prioritising one's profession is crucial, and exploring stock market investment can be considered at a later stage.

So, what should be the next step? Do you need some clarification? How does one actually go about becoming rich? These questions bother the average person who works hard for their money. It's understandable why someone might hesitate to invest their hard-earned money in a place where the things are so volatile that they could either strike a person millionaire or looser, everything in the blink of an eye. This is why only **3% of the Indian population**[ix] invests in the stock market (this is before COVID-19), compared to 13% of the Chinese population and 55% of the US population.

Middle-Class Dilemma

The stock market can be volatile and confusing for those who are not well-informed, leading many to seek safer investment options such as fixed deposits (FDs), gold, silver, real estate, Public Provident Fund (PPF), or government bonds. Real estate and gold/silver are tangible assets that provide a sense of security. Owning a piece of land, a home and gold/silver is often emotionally significant for middle-class families, and they are considered real investments. Many individuals, particularly homemakers, feel more secure with enough gold/silver ornaments, which they often pass down to their daughters or daughters-in-law. However, if a person owns more than one house and many gold/silver ornaments, they may have too many non-liquid assets. While these assets hold value, they do not generate significant returns and can be difficult to sell quickly.

Due to the volatility of the stock market, fewer people in India directly invest in stocks. Many individuals lack sufficient investment knowledge, making them vulnerable to being misled by others who exploit their desire to become wealthy. Bank officials, mutual fund advisors, and insurance agents may hound you if they learn that you have funds to invest. From their perspective, they are also working to earn a living by influencing you. However, we must have our own investment knowledge as it is our hard-earned money. These professionals may guide you based on their interests rather than your profit. It's crucial for us to be informed about investing our money in a relatively safe place with calculated risk, where it also has the potential to grow. I will explain the narrative created by investment agents and the psychological perspective behind these investments.

Fixed Deposits

This tool has been created for conservative investors who want to earn slightly better returns than a savings account. It is designed for middle-class individuals who are careful about spending and focused on meeting their personal and social responsibilities. These individuals have everyday financial obligations such as providing food for their family, owning a vehicle, buying or building a home, educating and marrying their children, and planning for a secure and comfortable retirement. They prioritise the safety and well-being of their family throughout their lives, and each aspect of the tool is connected to fulfilling their basic needs, including food, clothing, and housing.

Bank officials often encourage middle-class individuals to invest in Fixed Deposits (FDs) by promoting the security of the principal amount and the fixed returns offered. However, only a few people question the impact of inflation on the interest rate earned from FDs. While long-term FDs may provide slightly higher returns as compared to short-term FDs, these returns may not be enough to combat inflation. Another drawback of FDs is that tax is deducted at the highest income tax slab, meaning that even if someone earns a 6 to 7% return on FDs, the final amount after maturity could be around 4 to 5%. This is comparable to the return from a savings account. With a 4 to 5% return, money can actually lose value over time due to inflation.

Fixed Deposits (FDs) are a reliable option for temporary money parking, thanks to their easy liquidity. However, for those seeking slightly better returns, consider the potential of debt mutual funds. Debt mutual funds, like any other mutual fund scheme, have a volatility factor and cannot guarantee fixed returns. Therefore, one's investment horizon and need should determine the type of investment to make. By diversifying your investments, you can foster a sense of optimism about your financial growth. Additionally, an auto sweep-in facility in your bank account can help you make the most of your funds, depositing any excess as an FD.

Insurance/ Retirement plans, Unit Linked Insurance Policies (ULIPs) and Mutual Funds

Financial experts have developed various investment tools to assist middle-class individuals and small investors. These tools include insurance plans, retirement plans, unit-linked insurance policies (ULIP), and mutual funds. Their sales pitch revolves around targeting the concerns of middle-class people, such as funding for their children's education and marriages, post-retirement funds, medical expenses, and life insurance. They often emphasise the volatility of the stock market and the uncertainties of life to create a sense of urgency. Moreover, they may try to sell extended schemes that could last until you are 80 years old, making it easy for some to overlook the benefits of these schemes.

Some insurance companies have crores of money in their kitty as **unclaimed money**[x]. A while ago, I came across an article about LIC stating that they have over 21,539 Crores of unclaimed funds. With this much money, LIC could fund three 'Chandrayaan missions' and even imprint their logo on the moon's surface. It's worth noting that this substantial wealth has been accumulated using their customers' money. When financial experts or company representatives come to sell schemes, they often focus on the safety of your children, your post-retirement life, and life after you rather than explaining the rate of return on your investment or whether it is inflation-adjusted. They also avoid explaining the total returns on the scheme's maturity.

In many cases, the maturity of schemes yields minimal returns, while they use persuasive narratives or generate fear to sell their products. They often provide figures that captivate us without explaining the compounded interest rate or annual growth rate (CAGR). It's important to understand that no one is doing charity here; everyone aims to earn substantial wealth and become rich in the shortest possible time. There are no free lunches in the financial world.

Today, I received a call from an investment agency. The representative suggested a plan where I would invest Rs. 1 lakh per year for 12 years. After the 12th year, the company would pay approximately Rs. 1.25 lakh per year for the next 30 years, in addition to returning my accumulated sum of Rs. 12 lakh at the end of the 30 years. This scheme seems impressive as the investor would receive roughly 50 lakh by the end of 30 years.

Instead of opting for the scheme offered by the investment agent, consider investing 1 Lakh per year for 12 years. At a 12% Compound Annual Growth Rate (CAGR), this investment would grow to 27 Lakhs. If you reinvest this 27 Lakhs as a lump sum for 30 years, it could grow to approximately 8 Crore 10 Lakhs with a 12% CAGR and 18 Crore with a 15% CAGR. Comparing this to the agent's scheme, which would be a better option? I can explain how to achieve a 12% return without much hassle. Expecting a 12% to 15% rate of return over 30 years is achievable. Understanding the long-term rate of return and the accumulated sum is essential. Let me tell you about the magic of compounding. We often hear about uncertainties and fears, but with a long-term perspective and disciplined investing, one can create magic in one's life through the power of compounding. While short periods may be volatile, long-term investments can work miracles if one stays disciplined in investment.

Real Estate

Everyone, including animals, always dreams of having a home or a shelter, which is absolutely in sync with the law of nature. Everyone deserves a roof over their head, and there is no harm in investing in real estate. The process of buying a property is complicated and requires effort. There are always chances of fraud when we go for a property. Real estate dealers sell dream houses. They can even sell a godforsaken land in deep jungles in the name of some upcoming city with world-class facilities and what not. They will create a big entrance gate for their upcoming society, a broad road, some arboriculture, and a model house. Such schemes generally lure many middle-class salaried families into the trap of having their own sweet home, and many have lost their hard-earned money. Dealers have promised to deliver projects in 3 to 4 years. However, projects are almost dead even after ten years, with just 20 to 25% of work completed. Some middle-class families were shown dreams of their money becoming two times in 3 to 4 years after the project. I am not talking about only small builders; even big, renowned builders have become defaulters. The real problem comes when we start investing in real estate to earn money and take loans to buy property. Like any other investment, this investment also requires lots of knowledge and patience. This kind of investment does not offer liquidity very quickly. Sometimes, one may be stuck in a bad deal for years and may not even earn rates of return equivalent to FDs. Real estate properties are sometimes engulfed in legal issues and become a headache for life.

One significant issue is that financial institutions/banks encourage individuals to take out home loans or loans to buy land and portray it as an investment. However, any kind of loan can be a trap. While home loans offer benefits in terms of rebates in income tax, it's important to remember that these benefits may not always be helpful if the property has been purchased on loan. Buying a home on loan may be beneficial only when one plans to move into his home rather than keeping it on rent. The average growth in real estate is 9 to 10% per annum, but this average growth depends on the property's location. Sometimes, the returns on properties may even be lower than those from fixed deposits. Home loans are available at 8.0% to 10.0%[xi] on reducing the loan amount. With registry and property dealer costs involved, it is wise to take a home loan and buy a house if one has to move into that house immediately. Otherwise, as an investment, it may not provide adequate returns.

I purchased a plot in Agra (Uttar Pradesh) in the year 2011 for Rs 15 lakh, financed through a 10% interest rate loan. The plot was part of an upcoming project by a well-known builder, with an expected completion time of 4 to 5 years. I paid a monthly EMI of Rs 11,500 and cleared the loan in 2022. However, even after almost 11 years, the project is still less than 25% complete. I am still waiting for a buyer willing to pay even Rs 25 lakhs for the plot. If I had invested the money I spent on EMIs in an index fund or ETF with a 12% return rate, my wealth would now be around Rs 32 lakhs. This experience has taught me that buying property on loan for investment can be detrimental, especially when dealing with such projects.

Many people purchase apartments valued at Rs 1.5 to 2 crore by taking out loans. Once they possess the property, they put it up for rent. However, investing in such expensive property only pays off if the rental income covers the entire loan EMI. Real estate investments require a large amount of money. It's not possible to buy property with just a few thousand rupees. On the other hand, one can invest in stocks, mutual funds, index funds, or ETFs with just a few hundred to a few thousand rupees. Real estate is a good investment, but it comes with a few conditions: -

- After buying a house, it's recommended that the individual uses it as their primary residence. While it can be seen as an investment, the potential return on investment may be lower compared to other investment options.

- When considering real estate investments, it's prudent to explore commercial properties as an option. Compared to investing in multiple residential properties such as houses or flats, commercial properties have the potential to yield higher rental income and offer better overall growth returns.

- Always remember the importance of conducting comprehensive research and analysis of the area, whether dealing with residential or commercial property. Your in-depth understanding of the local market and community will be crucial in effectively managing the property over the long term.

- To effectively handle any potential legal issues, it is crucial to be financially and mentally prepared. Being well-prepared will empower you to navigate these challenges confidently when they arise.

- Before deciding to invest in plots using a loan, it is crucial to analyse the project's growth prospects thoroughly. Potential investors should meticulously compute the rate of return, interest rate, and government fees to make a well-informed and prudent decision.

- Instead of investing directly in real estate, consider investing in Index Funds or Exchange-Traded Funds (ETFs). These options can offer higher returns and greater liquidity over an extended period. When considering purchasing property, it's advisable to do so only when the project is at least 75% complete. Even if property rates rise, your capital may experience better growth in an index fund or ETF.

- Rental income is typically more lucrative when investing in property in metropolitan areas due to high demand. However, in non-metro areas, if the property is purchased using a loan, the potential for incurring financial losses increases.

- Generating more than 12% returns through the consistent acquisition and sale of properties is achievable for certain individuals. Nevertheless, it's crucial to recognise that this pursuit necessitates a substantial amount of time, effort, energy and unwavering dedication, requiring an earnest and wholehearted approach as if managing a business. It's not everybody's cup of tea to manage issues related to property buying and selling.

Gold/ Silver

Unlike paper currency, investing in gold and silver provides a tangible asset with intrinsic value. These metals are popular investment choices due to their physical visibility and value. However, before investing, it's essential to consider the rate of return, liquidity, physical safety, and making charges. Gold and silver can be a diversifying option, reducing the risk of having all your investments in one place. It's essential to be cautious and invest during market dips. While gold and silver can be used for availing a loan, they are not easily liquidated for cash. One cannot go to market to buy a car or a house with gold coins. Gold is often reinvested by purchasing new ornaments, coins, or bars. Furthermore, due to safety concerns, many investors store their gold and silver ornaments and assets in bank lockers. Therefore, these investments become dead assets, and using them for everyday transactions is challenging. Investing in gold bonds (SGBs) or gold ETFs is a better option as they address the issue of safeguarding the investment. The only advantage of this investment is its versatility for social functions, as it can be worn and used.

Though gold may give a 15% growth rate in the long run, after reducing making charges and government taxes, it will be less than 15% on any day. A retail investor will always face the problem of liquidity when exchanging gold for cash and the exchange rate may further reduce total returns. Therefore, it's advisable that gold and silver investments should not exceed 20-25% of your portfolio.

Index Funds/ Exchange-Traded Funds (ETFs)

Over 5,000 companies are listed in the Indian stock market. Based on their market cap, they are categorised into three broad categories: Large, Medium, and Small Capital companies. Broadly, **Large-cap companies**[xii] **have a market cap of Rs 20,000 crore or more. The market cap of mid-cap companies** is between **Rs 20,000 crore and Rs 5,000 crore. Small-cap companies have a market cap of below Rs 5,000 crore.** When an individual, broker, or finance company buys or sells stocks of any listed company, it is called direct stock buying or selling. However, when an individual invests in a group of stocks based on market indices, it is called index funds. These index funds could be exchange-traded funds (ETFs) or Index Mutual funds. Index Mutual funds can be purchased through mutual fund houses; no Demat account is required to buy a mutual fund. However, a Demat or trading account is needed to buy an ETF.

Index funds are incredibly popular and trendy investments because they are simple, low-cost, and offer diversification benefits. Both index mutual funds and ETFs aim to replicate the performance of an underlying index made up of stocks without the need for expensive portfolio managers and teams of analysts. It's essential to understand the basics of index mutual funds and ETFs before delving into the types of these funds. These funds attempt to mirror the performance of specific stock market indices, such as the Nifty 50, Nifty Midcap, or Nifty Bank. The weightage of the stocks in these funds is the same as the proportion of each stock in the index. For example, in the Indian market, these funds include: -

Type of Funds	Remarks
Nifty 50	First 50 companies on the National Index (Nifty)
Nifty Mid Cap 50	First 50 companies on the National Midcap Index (Nifty)
Nifty Small Cap 50	First 50 companies on the National Midcap Index (Nifty)
Gold ETF	Gold exchange traded fund. It represents physical gold bars that are 99.5% pure. One unit of gold ETF is equal to one gram of gold.

Nifty 50 (through Index MF or ETF)

The Nifty 50 is a benchmark index that monitors the performance of the top 50 large-cap stocks traded on the National Stock Exchange of India (NSE). Nifty 50 ETF is a personal favourite of mine. One might wonder why it's my favourite, considering it is also market-dependent. The simple answer is that when investing in Nifty 50 ETF, one invests in the fifty best large-cap companies of the Indian National Stock Exchange. **Large-cap funds invest mainly in the stocks of large-cap companies, also known as blue-chip companies.**

The Nifty 50 index comprises India's top 50 large-cap companies, with a combined market capitalisation of 15,451,822.90 crore. These companies play a crucial role in the Indian economy. Investing in the Nifty 50 index allows you to access a diversified portfolio of the country's top 50 companies. If any company underperforms, it is replaced by the 51st company in line. The performance of this group is indicative of the overall health of the national economy and the market's major players. Generally, this group performs well in the long term, barring any significant economic crises at the national or global level.

The second advantage is that you don't have to choose a specific company or sector to invest in. Even if you don't understand the stock market, investing in index funds/ ETFs can yield good returns in the long term (more than ten years). **Young professionals should consider Nifty 50, as the investment horizon is generally long, and knowledge about the stock market is usually limited.** Therefore, ETFs or Index Funds are known as straightforward investment options. In the long run, these funds can offer better returns than FDs, gold, bonds, or real estate. In a growing economy like India, these funds are likely to perform well and can provide compounded returns of 12 to 15%. By investing in these funds means you don't have to time the stock market. You may continue investing regularly even without extensive knowledge.

It's crucial to begin your investment journey by putting your money into index funds or ETFs. As you develop a better understanding of the stock market, you can expand your investment portfolio to suit your specific needs and expertise. While individual stocks can potentially lose all their value, index investing minimises this risk. **If a national index were to drop to zero, it would signify a complete economic collapse in the country.** Over the long run (10 to 20 years), Nifty 50 has given 12 to 15% of CAGR[xiii].

It is often seen that almost 50% of small-cap companies go bankrupt during a major market crash or crisis. Therefore, as a young investor, it is advisable to avoid investing in small-cap index funds, even though they may seem attractive due to their potential for good returns. For the first five years of your investment journey, it is recommended to limit your investments to Nifty 50 or Large-cap ETF. This approach is considered the safest option, especially in a highly volatile market. Investing in Nifty 50 can provide you with a good balance of risk and returns, putting you on the right investment path.

It's often suggested that you invest directly in stocks, or you might be enticed by the appeal of high-performing stocks or penny stocks due to their past performance. However, it's best to resist these temptations. Many inexperienced investors have been negatively impacted by the desire to earn more, leading to fear and negative sentiments about the stock market among the general public. Individual stock purchases by young retail investors, who generally lack sufficient knowledge, have historically resulted in low profits, especially when influenced by recommendations from friends or brokers. There have been cases where young investors have lost their hard-earned money in direct stock buying.

It is essential to first prioritise stability and establish a habit of regular investing without being overly focused on immediate results. After gaining experience and observing market fluctuations, consider investing a portion of your portfolio in individual stocks. However, be prepared for potential failures and losses, as predicting the market's movement is impossible. While some stocks may yield high returns, others may result in losses. Even in the long term, investing in individual stocks may not offer more than an average return of 18 to 20%. Therefore, opting for index investing and steady growth, rather than taking unnecessary risks, is wiser. If you still want to invest in stocks directly, choose large or medium-cap companies and intend to invest for the long term.

Mutual Funds

Mutual funds are diversified and not tied to a single index. They consist of a variety of stocks in a portfolio developed around different themes and sectors. Selecting a good mutual fund is a challenging task as these investments are market-dependent and can be volatile. While many people base their mutual fund purchases on past performance, it's important to note that past results do not guarantee future returns. The portfolio manager's skills, knowledge, and foresight influence a mutual fund's performance. There's a well-known saying in the mutual fund industry that **winners may not always stay winners**. Some mutual funds may perform poorly in the long run due to technological changes or specific sector requirements. Therefore, it's essential to be cautious when choosing mutual funds.

Additionally, mutual fund managers charge for their services, known as the expense ratio, and an exit load when you withdraw your money. As a result, profits earned from mutual funds are reduced due to these charges. When evaluating potential mutual fund investments, it's essential to consider the expense ratio and exit load as part of the rate of return calculation. Furthermore, the past performance advertised in a mutual fund brochure does not reflect the expense ratio and exit load. The Compound Annual Growth Rate (CAGR) shown for a particular mutual fund will be lower than advertised due to the deduction of the expense ratio and exit load.

Lump sum Investment Vs Systematic Investment Plan (SIP)

If an individual receives a lump sum of money from any source, such as a bonus, policy maturity, or a gift from a family member, investing the lump sum amount at the right time and for the long term can result in better returns. However, if an individual wants to develop the habit of investing without having a large sum of money at once, they should consider a systematic investment plan (SIP). SIP helps in becoming a disciplined investor without trying to time the market. It is a great way to invest regularly and spread out investments to average market fluctuations. One can start investing with as little as Rs 500 per month. Diversifying investments across two to five SIP schemes is essential to guard against losses in a single scheme.

Spending and Investing Wisely

Let's consider an example to understand it better. All the figures I am using to explain are only indicative and as of 2024. Suppose your monthly salary or earnings are Rs 1.5 lakhs, and your take-home salary is Rs 1.2 lakhs. Now, you want to buy an SUV costing Rs 22 lakhs. You made a down payment of Rs 5 lakhs and paid the rest through a loan. If you take a loan of Rs 17 lakhs at an interest rate of 10% for ten years, your EMI will be approximately Rs 22,500, and you will pay a total interest of Rs 10 lakhs on the principal amount. After ten years, your car will have cost you Rs 32 lakhs, but its value will hardly be Rs 10 lakhs due to depreciation.

If you had chosen a standard hatchback car priced at around Rs 10 lakhs instead of an SUV and made a down payment of Rs 5 lakhs with a loan of Rs 5 lakhs at the same interest rate and duration, the total cost of the car over ten years would have been approximately Rs 12,92,000. Your monthly EMI would have decreased to Rs 6,600 from Rs 22,500, resulting in a monthly saving of about Rs 16,000. I assumed you could have managed an EMI of Rs 22,500 with your salary of Rs 1.2 lakhs. **Now, there is a twist in the story**.

If you had chosen a hatchback car using the same budget I mentioned earlier, you could afford an EMI of Rs 22,500 and save around Rs 16,000 per month for ten years. It would be wise to invest this amount in Nifty 50 (a national Index) ETF for ten years. Considering the potential lack of expertise in the stock market and staying away from higher risks, I have selected Nifty 50 for you as a simple and reliable investment option. Based on the Nifty 50's returns over the last 20 years, it could provide a 12 to 15% return over ten years. Therefore, your monthly investment of Rs 16,000 in Nifty 50 at an approximate 13% rate of return could yield you around Rs 35 lakhs in 10 years. Even after adjusting for 6% inflation, this amount would still be about Rs 27 lakhs.

After ten years, you can sell your hatchback for 5 lakhs, and you will have a total of Rs 27 + 5 = 32 lakhs inflation-adjusted money in your hand. You can buy a high-class SUV with your own money.

If you had chosen to buy a pre-owned car for Rs 5 lakhs instead of purchasing a new hatchback and invested Rs 22,500 every month for ten years in Nifty 50, you would have received approximately Rs 37 lakhs after adjusting for inflation.

I have simplified all these calculations to emphasise the importance of spending and investing wisely. This example can be applied anywhere to understand the value of money and the significance of making sensible investments and prudent spending decisions. You can use this example to plan your needs by effectively utilising your resources. The point that I am trying to convey is that **young professionals should avoid taking loans to improve their lifestyle**. Each of us needs to be patient enough to earn money, invest it wisely, allow it to grow, and gradually strive to add value to our lifestyle. Remember that as you step into your professional life, you are at the beginning of a long journey. You have many years ahead to work towards and enjoy your desired lifestyle. By cultivating patience and making intelligent use of time to invest and grow your money wisely, you will experience substantial progress and positive changes in the years ahead. Getting into a cycle of debt in the early years of your life will keep you in debt for a long time. Therefore, learn to invest before making plans to spend.

Power of Compounding

In 8th grade, we are typically introduced to simple and compound interest. While we learn the basic concepts, we need to delve deeper into the concept of compounding. Rather than simply memorising formulas and solving problems. Our education system should focus on helping us understand the practical implications of these formulas in growing our money. Let me share a great example that illustrates the power of compounding, which I came across while learning about it through social media.

Say you have a mug with some bacteria in it, which can double in number every second. After 10 seconds, the mug is half full of bacteria. How long will it take for the mug to be full of bacteria? The answer is that it will only take one more second for the mug to be full of bacteria. This is because the bacteria double themselves every second, so on the 11th second; the mug will be full of bacteria. The same principle applies to investments - after a certain point, money can proliferate. Many people lose patience with their investments in the early stages and withdraw their money prematurely, missing out on the potential for significant growth. While reaching the first million is challenging; however, doubling or tripling that amount once you've achieved it becomes easier.

Time is one of the most critical factors in compounding. Compounding has the power to generate exponential growth if one remains invested for a longer period. Therefore, **it is crucial to start investing at a young age**. The earlier you start investing, the larger your investment can grow. **The Nifty 50 index delivered a compound annual growth rate (CAGR)[xiv] of 14 per cent in the last ten years and 14.9% in the last 20 years**.

I wish I had known this when you were born. If I had invested Rs. 1 lakh in Nifty 50 when you were born in 2002, this money would have grown to approximately Rs. 18,82,152 by 2023 (after 21 years), which could have helped with your higher studies. If I had left the money invested for another ten years, it would have grown to Rs. 76,14,353 by 2033 with an annualised return of 15%. If I had remained invested until 2043 (41 years), the one lakh would have become Rs. 3,08,04,308.

Can you see the magic of compounding over the last 10 and 20 years with the same rate of return? Now, compare this calculation with the bacteria riddle. In the riddle, magic happened at the 11th and 12th second, and similarly here, magic happened in the 31st and 41st year. From 21 years to 31 years of investment, one lakh rupees grows from approximately 18 lakhs to 76 lakhs, and by the 41st year, it grows to 3 crore plus.

The concept of compounding, wherein the interest earned on an investment is reinvested to generate further earnings, coupled with the practice of early investing and remaining invested for the long term, can lead to remarkable financial growth. When an individual starts investing early and allows their investments to grow over time, even a modest initial investment has the potential to grow into significant wealth due to the compounding effect. This principle not only holds true for financial wealth but also for personal development. By consistently dedicating time and effort to personal growth over an extended period, one can witness the incredible transformation and results.

This example powerfully illustrates the value of maintaining consistency during the early stages of one's career, whether it pertains to increasing earnings, effectively managing expenses, or making smart investments. By staying committed to these principles over time, individuals can lay a strong foundation for future financial security and personal growth.

Suppose you read just ten pages per day of any self-help, science, economics, psychology or other good book. In that case, you can finish approximately 18 books in a year (considering the average book has 200 pages). Just imagine the knowledge you will gain after a year! For example, if you are weak in understanding investing principles and have read 18 books on personal finance and investment in a year, no one will be able to beat you in personal finance by the end of the year. You won't need a financial expert for your investments. Remember, **great things do not happen overnight; they occur over time with consistency, discipline, and patience**.

If wealth creation is so simple, you might wonder why more people don't use this method to become millionaires. You're right to think that way. There are two main reasons why we don't become rich: first, we need help to grasp the power of compounding, and second, we need more patience to stay invested for the long term, even though we understand its importance. We get scared when we see our investments fluctuate. Staying invested for 20-25 years is a long time and requires a good understanding of compounding and patience. On a lighter note, one could stay invested for an extended period if they suffer from memory loss after investing and regain their memory after 40 years. They would become a millionaire once they get their memory back. Now, jokes apart, I invested Rs 2.35 Lakhs in 2011, and I forgot. Just a year back, I saw it and found that it has given a CAGR of 16.98%, and its current value is Rs 16.17 Lakhs.

Future Value (fv) and Present Value (pv) Formulae

One thing I learnt very late in my life is about the "Future value" (fv) and "Present value" (pv) formulas. You don't have to know the derivation of these formulas, but anyone can easily use them to plan their finances. These formulas have been designed beautifully, and their usage can be astonishing when planning your future goals. I wish someone had told me or taught me about the uses of these formulas when I was in 10th grade; I would have become a millionaire or billionaire by now. Sometimes, I feel it is some kind of conspiracy as no one teaches us investment tools at the right age. Simple and compound interest are introduced like any other chapter in Mathematics. These formulas explain the power of compounding, which can help define your financial goals. I have used the future value formula while illustrating car purchase examples. You can find calculators for future value and present value formulas on Google. Otherwise, you can use them on MS Excel worksheets. I can explain how to use these formulas on an MS Excel worksheet. Let's try and understand these formulas.

Future Value (fv)

In simple terms, **determining the future value of your investment over time with a specific interest rate is known as the 'future value' of your present money**. You can invest money in a lump sum or in installments. The future value (fv) formula is used in finance to calculate the future worth of an investment or sum of money after a certain period, assuming a fixed interest rate and compounding frequency. This formula calculates your total investment with interest compounding every year and demonstrates the power of compounding.

You can plan many financial goals in your life with this formula. One can simply use the fv formula to calculate the future worth of his money: -

Formula for Future Value (FV):

FV=PV×(1+r/n)(n∗t)FV=PV×(1+r/n)(n∗t)

Where:

- **FV** is the future value of the investment.
- **PV** is the present or initial principal amount.
- **r** is the annual interest rate (expressed as a decimal).
- **n** is the number of times that interest is compounded per year.
- **t** is the number of years the money is invested.

FV through MS Excel Work Sheet

Let's understand the future value (FV) formula using an MS Excel worksheet and learn how to use it. To use the FV formula, simply type =FV in any cell of an Excel sheet, open a small bracket and then input the required values. Once you've entered the values, close the bracket and press Enter to get the result.

=fv(rate,nper,pmt,[pv],[type])

where,

fv = future value/ worth of money

rate = interest rate per period e.g. annual rate of interest nper = No of payment periods or Compounding frequency or in number of installments one is going to invest i.e. how many years one is going to stay invested.

pmt = Payment made in each period or installment amount per period (monthly or yearly investment amount)

pv = present value or initial investment amount (lump sum)

type = Specifies when payments are due. 0 or omitted means payments are due at the end of the period, while 1 means payments are due at the beginning of the period (e.g. start of the month or year).

Let's consider an example to help you understand these formulas using an MS Excel worksheet. After getting a job, you saved Rs 20,000 monthly and started investing. For the first three years, you invested this money each month for three years in the national index through the Nifty 50 ETF. Let's calculate how much money you will accumulate if you receive a humble 12% annualised return.

=fv(rate,nper,pmt,[pv],[type])

=fv(12%,3,(20000x12),0,1)

=fv(12%,3,240000,0,1)

=9,07,038.00/-

After three years, you will accumulate Rs 9,07,038.00 by investing Rs 20,000 per month, assuming an annualised return of 12%. Since this calculation does not involve a lump sum investment and only Rs 20,000 per month is invested, I have kept the present value (PV) as zero and pmt as 20,000x12.

At this juncture, consider getting a car if you don't have one already. Alternatively, you could continue using your bike and invest the money in furthering your education, such as pursuing an MBA or obtaining another qualification. The key to financial success lies in having a vision, setting life goals, and learning to invest based on those goals. Some people live without planning for the future and invest whatever money is left after their expenses. However, a more innovative approach would be to prepare for future goals and expenses based on your vision and then regularly invest to achieve those goals. One can quickly achieve financial goals by avoiding unplanned expenses and consistently investing.

Financial Planning and Budgeting

To achieve financial success, it is crucial to have a well-defined vision. This vision should encompass short-term (30-year), mid-term (45-year), and long-term (60-year) financial goals. Effective financial management involves more than just budgeting and investing. It requires strategic planning that balances both saving and spending. Understanding your income in relation to your short and long-term financial needs is essential. Developing an investment plan before making any significant expenditure is critical. This involves breaking down your financial goals into manageable phases and allocating funds accordingly. By practicing restraint in spending during the early stages of your career, you can lay a strong foundation for building wealth in the future.

Wealth is not solely about increasing one's income; it also involves making intelligent spending choices and wise investment decisions. At this point, it's essential to understand the significance of financial planning and acquire some knowledge about investing. Let's take a moment to consider some significant milestones in life and how they intersect with financial planning.

In college, many aspire to secure a good job, earn a decent salary, and eventually own a car and a home. As we transition into the workforce and embark on a new stage in life, we often find ourselves desiring various possessions such as phones, laptops, televisions, refrigerators, microwaves, washing machines, furniture, decorations, bicycles, cars, and homes. While it's natural to have such desires, it's essential to recognise that there's no rush to acquire all of these items within the first year of our careers. Some of these possessions can be managed without, and it's perfectly acceptable to gradually fulfill these desires or needs based on their priority level.

As thoughtful individuals, it is essential to carefully categorise our needs into three distinct parts: **Vital, Essential, and Desirable**. "Vital requirements" encompass items that are indispensable for daily life and basic sustenance, such as smart-phones and laptops. Smart-phones play a critical role in communication, online shopping, and banking, while a computer (Laptop) may be essential for professional work and personal organisation. The "essential list" comprises items like televisions, refrigerators, and washing machines, which significantly contribute to our quality of life but are not considered vital for survival. As one begins their career, owning a house is often categorised as "desirable." The categorisation of items should be based on one's available salary and financial circumstances.

When compiling the "Vital List," weighing the option of purchasing refurbished or medium-category items is essential. This approach enables efficient allocation of available resources and strategic investment of savings for the future. For instance, instead of overspending on a high-end car, it could be financially astute to initially opt for a more affordable vehicle with the plan to upgrade later. Considering the relatively short lifespan of electronic devices, it may not be advisable to splurge on high-end items. Renting certain items also offers financial flexibility, serving as a safety net, especially when starting a career.

Let's consider a scenario to gain a better understanding. Imagine you start a job in 2025 with a monthly salary of Rs 1.5 Lakhs. After mandatory deductions, your take-home pay is Rs 1.2

Lakhs. It's essential to keep your expenses minimal in the first few years and maximise your investments. **If your take-home pay is less, focus on reducing expenses rather than reducing investments.** For the initial five years of your career, prioritise investing and limit your spending to essential items. Even certain essential expenses can be postponed and planned after the first five years of your career. Let's create a monthly budget for you for the first five years.

Item	Expenditure per Month	Remarks
House Rent	Rs 25000	For a two BHK
Grocery	Rs 10000	
Maid	Rs 5000	
Transport/ Petrol	Rs 5000	
Leisure	Rs 10000	if you plan to have party every weekend
Health	Rs 5000	Includes your EMI for health insurance
Misc	Rs 10000	Includes your EMI for term insurance or savings for up-skilling yourself
Total	Rs 70000/-	This is rough monthly expenditure
Balance	Rs 50000/-	Amount left for investing

You can save more money by working from home. Consider living in a hostel or sharing a place to reduce house rent until you are single.

I am confident that you are a disciplined investor and were able to invest Rs 50,000 per month. While a sum of Rs 50,000 investment may seem like a lot initially, as your salary increases, it will become more manageable in the long run. Out of this Rs 50,000, you kept investing Rs 30,000 until 2045 (i.e. for 20 years) and the remaining Rs 20,000 until 2030 (i.e., five years). For your long-term investment, i.e. 20 years, you could get a 15% annualised return; for your short-term investment, i.e. five years, you could get a 12% rate of return.

Let's start by calculating the long-term benefits of your investment.

Long term investment (Rs 30,000 per month): -

Let's calculate your wealth in 20 years with a 15% annual return on your long-term investment.

=fv(rate,nper,pmt,[pv],[type])

=fv(15%,20,(30000x12),0,1)

= Rs 4,24,11,643

Short-term investment (Rs 20,000 per month): -

Let's calculate your wealth after five years with a 12% annual return on your short-term investment.

=fv(rate,nper,pmt,[pv],[type])

=fv(12%,5,(20000x12),0,1)

=Rs 17,07,645

Over the next five years, you will accumulate 17 lakhs with your short term investment. You can use this money to establish your home and purchase a hatchback car. These five years of disciplined living will result in a significant return. Therefore, the initial five years of your career are crucial for professional advancement and financial growth. During this period, you should focus on enhancing your professional skills. Immerse yourself in your profession – dedicate your time and energy to it. Sharpen your expertise so that you can experience substantial growth after five years. Like long-term investments, your knowledge will grow exponentially if you refine your skills and acquire new knowledge. Similarly, living within your means and reducing expenses during the first five years, you can earn enough money to kick-start your life.

Even after five years, continue investing. Set new targets and invest Rs 20,000 or more for the next five years to reach a short-term target. You can increase your EMI (estimated monthly investment) instead of spending on luxuries. Invest more in essentials and create money for your luxuries. Avoid depending on credit cards and loans. Remember, the initial goal of reaching first one crore is the most challenging. After that, money compounds very fast. As a salaried individual, your income may not grow exponentially. Therefore, you will need to manage your expenditures to invest more.

Some knowledgeable people will question **inflation (Prices of goods and services increase with time due to various factors. This increase in prices of goods and services is known as inflation)** and its effect on your accumulated wealth. Calculating inflation-adjusted returns may sound complex, but it's actually quite straightforward. We can consider an average inflation rate of 6%. Using the same future value (fv) formula, you can adjust for inflation by subtracting the inflation rate from the expected annualised return. Therefore, the inflation-adjusted FV formula will be: -

=fv{(rate of return- inflation rate), nper, pmt, [pv], [type]}

Your inflation adjusted wealth will be: -

Investment	Without inflation adjustment	With inflation adjustment
Rs 30,000 per month for 20 years with 15% return	Rs 4, 24,11,643	Rs 2,56,55,451
Rs 20,000 per month for 5 years with 12% return	Rs 17,07,645	Rs 14,34,076

Even after adjusting your wealth for inflation, you will still have substantial wealth. This depends on how disciplined you are in saving and investing your money wisely. Instead of waiting for a salary increase, you can increase it by saving a few hundred rupees and investing it in the right place. You must have understood the power of compounding and wealth creation by now. Let's now discuss the 'Present Value' formula.

Present Value (pv)

The present value (PV) formula can be used to calculate the present value of an investment. This formula helps us understand the current value of loan payments and the total cost of borrowing, including interest. Lenders can also use this to assess the loan's profitability. Individuals use present value calculations to determine the money needed to save for retirement or other goals by estimating future expenses and discounting them to their present value.

The present value formula, often denoted as PV in financial calculations, determines the current worth of money to be received or paid in the future. It is a fundamental concept in finance used in various financial and investment decisions. The formula for calculating the present value of a future cash flow is: -

PV=FV(1+r)nPV=(1+r)nFV

Where:

- **PV** = Present Value
- **FV** = Future Value (the amount of money to be received or paid in the future)
- **r** = Discount rate (the rate of return or interest rate used to discount the future cash flow)
- **n** = Number of periods (the number of time periods between the present and future cash flow)

PV through MS Excel Work Sheet

To understand the PV formula in MS Excel, type =pv in any Excel sheet cell and start with a small bracket. Then, input the required values and press the Enter key to get the result.

=pv(rate,nper,pmt,[fv],[type])

where,

- pv = present value of the forecasted sum
- rate = interest rate per period e.g. annual rate of interest
- nper = No of payment periods
- pmt = Payment made in each period or installment amount per period (for regular investment)
- fv = The future value or the value you want to calculate the present value for. If omitted, it's assumed to be 0.
- type = An optional argument that specifies whether payments are due at the beginning (1) or end (0) of the period. If omitted, it's assumed to be 0 (end of the period).

Let's consider an example to understand this concept better. Imagine a person anticipating needing Rs 50 lakhs for his child's higher education in 20 years. How much would this amount be worth today? What is the present value of Rs 50 lakhs in the year 2044? Will the person's current savings be sufficient for their child's future, or will they need to increase their savings? We can calculate all of this using a specific formula. Let's assume that the inflation rate is 6%.

=pv(rate,nper,pmt,[fv],[type])

= pv (6%,20,0,50,00000,1)

= 15,60,000/-

Please note that Today's Rs 15,60,000 will be equivalent to Rs 50 lakh after 20 years if the inflation rate remains 6%. Currently, the average cost of higher education is around 25 to 30 lakhs. Therefore, this individual needs to increase his investments to afford his child's education after 20 years.

Many of us believe that our investments are sufficient to support a comfortable retirement and achieve our future financial goals. However, it's essential to have a formula that can help us assess the adequacy of our savings. This formula serves as a reality check, prompting us to reconsider our investment and spending plans. By evaluating our future wealth objectives, this formula can guide us in determining whether a specific investment is adequate or if adjustments are needed.

When using the FV and PV functions in Excel, it is important to match the units for interest rate and period. If the interest rate is annual, the number of periods should also be in years, and the payment should be consistent with the frequency (e.g. annual, quarterly, or monthly).

Narrative about Stock Market

Investing in the stock market can be highly volatile and unpredictable due to various factors. Timing the stock market is challenging, even for experienced professionals. Company fundamentals, market sentiment, and external events influence stock prices. A single statement from a prominent individual, such as a political leader or business figure, can lead to significant market fluctuations. Major events like national elections and global affairs can also substantially impact stock prices. Because of its unpredictable nature, the stock market has often been compared to a ghost, elusive and mysterious. Many individuals learn about the complexities of the stock market from their parents, family friends or teachers.

Many people who receive a fixed salary experience a sense of unease regarding the stock market. This apprehension often stems from a lack of understanding and a fear of the market's perceived complexity and unpredictability. The prevailing narrative surrounding the stock market emphasises its failures rather than successes. However, similar to any professional field, attaining success in the stock market demands a comprehensive understanding of the national economy and familiarity with governmental policies, both domestically and internationally, that have the potential to impact a country's growth.

It is crucial to possess a fundamental understanding of how financial services operate within the country. While a deep dive into the intricacies of the stock market and financial services is beyond the scope of this book, I can offer valuable insights into key terms and definitions that will aid in deciphering stock market movements. Consider this a launching point, and commit to continuously expanding your knowledge about the stock market over time.

Deepen your understanding by exploring various books on personal finance. But don't limit yourself to just one format. Augment your financial management skills by consuming diverse content formats such as videos, podcasts, and articles. These resources, each with their unique perspectives and insights, will serve as valuable tools in your ongoing journey of understanding and mastering the stock market. By embracing a variety of learning resources, you can gain a more comprehensive understanding of the stock market and improve your financial management skills.

Becoming proficient in the stock market is akin to mastering a discipline such as computer science engineering. Successful navigation of the stock market requires a significant commitment to education and staying abreast of market developments. It's worthwhile to recognise that solely relying on a salary to accumulate wealth can be challenging. Pursuing alternative paths, such as entrepreneurship or business investment, becomes necessary. While entrepreneurship may not be feasible for everyone, investing in businesses through the stock market provides a more widely accessible avenue for wealth creation.

Let's familiarise ourselves with some definitions and jargon of the stock market.

The Boss of the Sahukars(Money Lenders)

The Reserve Bank of India (RBI) is the central bank of India, responsible for supervising and regulating all nationalised and private banks and the monetary systems in India. Its role in providing stability and growth to the Indian economy is crucial. The RBI acts as the supervisor of the Indian economy and takes all necessary measures to ensure a stable and growing economy. **It formulates and implements India's monetary policy and uses various tools such as the repo rate, reverse repo rate, cash reserve ratio (CRR), and statutory liquidity ratio (SLR)**

to control the money supply in the economy. RBI influences banks' lending and borrowing activities by adjusting these rates and ratios. Before we move further, let me explain the jargons mentioned above. One may skip reading these jargons if one don't want to complicate things; however, I would advice to read once for better understanding: -

- <u>Repo Rate</u> – *This is the interest rate charged by the RBI form banks when RBI is lending money to banks.*

- <u>Reverse Repo Rate</u> - *This is the interest rate at which the RBI borrows money from banks.* **This is always lower than the Repo rate.**

- <u>Cash Reserve Ratio (CRR)</u> – *As a regulatory authority, RBI directs all the banks to keep some money in liquid cash. This is kept with RBI as security money. RBI does not pay any interest on this money. Banks cannot use this money for lending or borrowing. Therefore, CRR or Cash Reserve Ratio is* **the percentage of a bank's total deposits that it needs to maintain as liquid cash with RBI.**

- <u>Statutory Liquidity Ratio (SLR)</u> – *Banks are supposed to maintain some liquidity so that they can fulfill requirements of customers if they want early liquidity. Statutory Liquidity Ratio or SLR is* **the minimum percentage of deposits that a commercial bank has to maintain in the form of liquid cash, gold or other securities.** *It is basically the reserve requirement that a bank is expected to keep before offering credit to customers. The SLR is fixed and imposed by the RBI and is a form of control over the credit growth in India. SLR plays a very important role in fixing the minimum rate at which a bank can lend money to its customers. This minimum amount is called the* **base rate.** *This helps in building transparency between the Reserve Bank of India and other public dealing banks.*

- <u>Base Rate</u> - Base rate is defined as **the minimum interest rate set by the RBI below which Indian banks are not permitted to lend to their customers**. *Unless there is a government mandate, the RBI rule specifies that no bank may offer loans at an interest rate lower than the base rate.*

The Reserve Bank of India (RBI) is an advisor and banker to central and state governments. Its primary responsibilities include: -

- Managing the government's accounts.
- Ensuring sufficient liquidity in the banking system.
- Controlling inflation.
- Fostering economic growth.

All commercial banks hold accounts with the RBI, which provides them with banking services and offers financial assistance during crises by lending money. The RBI also manages India's foreign exchange reserves and develops policies to stabilise the value of the Indian rupee. Additionally, the RBI plays a crucial role in developing the financial market, implementing reforms, and promoting the use of technology in financial management. It oversees payment and settlement systems in India, such as Real-Time Gross Settlement (RTGS), National Electronic Funds Transfer (NEFT), and Unified Payments Interface (UPI).

I'm sure I've confused you a lot by now. You must be wondering why I'm trying to explain the banking system in India. By the way, I'm not an economist. I've studied these terms to make you understand the basics, but I have no intention of teaching you macroeconomics.

By now, you must have understood who the boss of India's all banks and financial services is. Yes, it is the RBI. When an individual or a company needs money, they go to banks to borrow money. When banks need money, they go to the RBI. Therefore, we may call the RBI the bank of banks.

Let me summarise what I've said so far. The RBI provides loans to banks at an interest rate called the repo rate and borrows money from banks at an interest rate known as the reverse repo rate. Banks lend money to their customers at a minimum interest rate known as the 'Base Rate', which is determined by the RBI.

No bank operates solely for social service. While their role is to help people manage their finances and lend them money in times of crisis, but it is not provided for free. In the past, this role was fulfilled by "Sahukars" (money lenders), who would lend money to those in need, often taking valuable items such as ornaments or land as collateral. They would also charge specific interest rates. In modern times, banks have taken over the role of Sahukars, but with a key difference. Unlike the unregulated Sahukars, banks are now governed by the RBI (Reserve Bank of India) to prevent exploitation and ensure standard operating procedures. Banks could have operated similarly to the Sahukars without the RBI's oversight. Therefore, the RBI can be seen as the regulator of the modern-day Sahukars. Its role is not only to control banks but also to have an overview of the country's economy.

Lending and Borrowing

After understanding the role and importance of the RBI, let's explore how the banking system functions. Commercial banks act as institutions for lending and borrowing. They make money by lending funds to those in need at an interest rate, similar to Sahukars. Without the RBI, banks could easily set their own rules and interest rates for lending, akin to Sahukars. The main distinction between banks and Sahukars is that Sahukars were money lenders who used their own wealth to lend and earn profits from the interest paid by borrowers. In contrast, banks' lending activities are funded by the money they receive from the general public as custodians. Banks serve as custodians for the general public's money and business companies holding accounts with them. Banks have become a means to circulate money from one party to another and earn interest.

The Reserve Bank of India (RBI) acts as a regulator to ensure that banks do not engage in risky behaviour and to maintain stability in the country. To achieve this, RBI requires banks to maintain a certain amount of security deposits, which is known as the Cash Reserve Ratio (CRR). This helps prevent banks from misusing public funds and keeps their activities in check. Additionally, RBI mandates banks to maintain a statutory liquidity ratio (SLR) to regulate and control the money supply in the economy. By imposing SLR, RBI can manage liquidity and control the economy's credit flow.

The Reserve Bank of India (RBI) can adjust the Statutory Liquidity Ratio (SLR) percentage as part of its monetary policy to control the money supply in the economy. When the RBI raises the SLR, banks must hold a higher proportion of their deposits in the form of liquid assets. This reduces their capacity to lend. On the other hand, when the RBI lowers the SLR, banks get more funds to lend, which may stimulate economic activity. SLR ensures that banks have a certain level of safety and stability by holding liquid assets that can be quickly converted into cash in times of financial stress or emergencies.

Banks typically maintain their reserves to lend money, but they sometimes need to borrow money from the RBI to meet urgent short-term needs. The RBI lends money to banks at the repo rate. When the repo rates increase, banks need to raise their lending rates to adjust. Simply put, banks will only lend money at higher rates than the repo rate to make a profit. When banks increase their lending rates, only those in need will borrow, leading to a reduction in borrowing and subsequently reducing the public's purchasing power. This results in less cash flow in the market and lower sales, indicating a slowdown in the market and potentially leading to stagnation or a downturn in the stock market (known as a bearish market).

When the RBI reduces repo rates, banks also decrease their lending rates, encouraging people to take out more loans. This increases the cash flow in the market, leading to higher demand. As a result, the public's buying capacity increases, creating a positive trend in the market and causing an upturn in the stock market (referred to as a bullish market).

The information provided is based on economic principles and observed market trends. Changes in repo rates typically influence whether the market becomes bullish or bearish. The Reserve Bank of India (RBI) manages cash flow in the market by controlling repo rates, the Cash Reserve Ratio (CRR), and the Statutory Liquidity Ratio (SLR). Lower cash flow reduces the demand for goods and services, which can slow down the economy and vice versa.

Let me tell you one more term. Net Demand and Time Liabilities (NDTL) are the total amount of money available to a bank for providing loans. They consist of all the deposits made to the bank by customers minus the amount that the bank has invested in other banks. In simpler terms, NDTL refers to the total demand and time liabilities (deposits) that the public holds with the banks. Demand deposits include all the liabilities that the bank must pay immediately on demand.

The Reserve Bank of India (RBI) has established the Cash Reserve Ratio (CRR) and Statutory Liquidity Ratio (SLR) to monitor and regulate banks. CRR is the proportion of funds banks must keep with the RBI as a security measure. SLR is designed to ensure that banks maintain enough liquidity and do not lend out all the funds accumulated from the public. CRR and SLR are calculated as a percentage of NDTL, as determined by the RBI from time to time. By maintaining SLR, banks are compelled to be able to return customers' money if they wish to withdraw it.

The key to a healthy economy is the circulation of money. This requires a balance between producers and consumers, with goods being produced and consumers available to purchase them. The continuous flow of money between individuals, businesses, and financial institutions helps maintain a stable cash flow in the market. Any imbalance in this cycle can lead to either a bearish or bullish market.

Consider a salaried individual as an example. When they receive their salary at the beginning of the month, they have a good amount of purchasing power (cash flow or liquidity). They go to the market and make purchases, but by the 15th of the month, they realise they have very little money left and start controlling their expenses. They restrict themselves to the essentials (limited cash flow or inadequate liquidity). This is why people save money for unexpected expenses or special occasions. They create a budget and save money using various methods. Some un-financially organised individuals take out loans to meet their needs. During holidays, some people exceed their budgets. They either use their saved money or take out loans. The additional cash flow in the market raises the prices of goods, and in economic terms, this is referred to as 'inflation'. I can share an anecdote if you'd like.

During Hindu religious festivals, the demand for eggs and chicken suddenly decreases as many people choose to be vegetarians for religious reasons. This change in dietary preference lasts for the duration of the festival, leading to a drop in prices for eggs and chicken. Once the festival ends, demand and prices for eggs and chicken increase. Conversely, fruit prices increase during the festive season due to increased demand as many people fast and use fruits to offer to God. This demonstrates how the prices of various items fluctuate based on demand during religious festivals.

It's important to remember that excess cash flow or liquidity in the market can lead to increased inflation over time. This excess cash flow is why the RBI regulates repo rates, CRR, and SLR to control inflation. However, during the COVID-19 pandemic, the opposite occurred. Due to the lockdown, goods sales were low, and cash flow was minimal. As a result, the government requested the RBI to help the public, especially small-scale business owners struggling to sustain their businesses. In response, the RBI reduced repo rates to inject liquidity into the market.

It's important to note the following points: The repo rate, CRR, SLR rate revisions, and inflation display specific patterns over time. The stock market movement is cyclical in the long run, resembling an irregular sine wave curve. It can move upwards, sideways, or downwards. **One of the factors influencing the stock market is changes in cash flow and this change in cash flow could be because of multiple reasons**. Following changes in repo rates, the market may exhibit erratic behaviour for a period of time. In the short term (say within six months), the market is volatile, but in the long term, it is influenced by stable government, government economic policies and the global economy. Events such as the COVID crisis or changes in geopolitical situations, such as the Russia-Ukraine war, can also impact stock markets due to factors like importing or exporting commodities to and from affected nations. The fear of the unknown outcome of a battle is also significant. This is why it's not advisable to enter the stock market without sufficient knowledge. It's important to understand that banks are keen on providing loans, while the government aims to control cash flow. Excessive cash flow and resource scarcity are critical factors in determining the economy's future. Anything in excess is detrimental, and this principle applies here also.

Loans, Credit Card- A Big Trap

In the past, people used to save money for months to buy a cycle or scooter. Government banks were reluctant to give loans and had complicated procedures. Then private banks and liberal economic policies emerged, and private banks started offering loans for education, cars, houses, trips, and personal loans for small functions or dinners. Nowadays, banks aggressively pursue customers to provide loans, even to the extent of calling them during odd hours (even when you are sleeping) and requiring minimal paperwork. They are willing to provide loans for any purpose, including personal, vehicle, marriage, education, or property loans.

Let's consider this: If taking loans is so beneficial, why don't bankers themselves take all the loans? Loans are a trap, and I have already explained why banks offer loans. In the olden days, farmers took loans from money lenders and remained in debt for generations. Please don't take any of the loans which I have mentioned above. Don't take loans if you cannot create assets from them. Don't take a loan to develop liabilities for yourself. I have suffered from taking various loans in my life. Banks create dreams for you and help you fulfill those dreams with their loans. You dream of an SUV worth Rs 20 Lakhs, and they will give you a loan with zero down payment. You just think of a home and banks will be ready to give you even a 1 Cr loan.

Let's consider example of a car to understand the situation better. Suppose you are interested in purchasing an SUV costing Rs 20 lakhs, and the car dealer offers you a loan with zero down payment. Excited about the offer, you have decided to take out a loan of Rs 20 lakhs for ten years, with an estimated monthly installment (EMI) of Rs 26000. However, it's important to remember that a car is a depreciating asset, and its value will significantly decrease over time. By committing to this loan, you may face financial strain as you'll need to cover maintenance, insurance, and running costs while the car's value depreciates.

Alternatively, if you had invested the same amount as the EMI (Rs 26000) in Nifty 50 for ten years at an approximate 12% return, you could have earned Rs 61,32,000/-. This is not to discourage you from enjoying life or making purchases but to highlight the importance of prioritising your financial decisions. **Consider delaying expenditures if they are not urgent and investing the money during that waiting period.**

I used to have various loans, including car, computer, property, and home loans. More than 50% of my salary would go towards repaying EMIs of these loans. Although my car is 14 years old and on its last legs, I was still paying off the car loan till recently. However, I'm happy to share that I paid off all my loans the previous week and am now debt-free. I wanted to clear my loans for a long time and live a more straightforward, stress-free life. I believe that taking loans for things like phones, cars, TVs, and property is a big mistake.

Similar to loans, a credit card can also be a significant pitfall. Many young professionals fall into this trap. When you're young, you often have more wants and fewer financial resources. In your early working years, you desire to own a large mobile phone, TV, car, and a luxuriously decorated house. You may even have a foreign holiday on your bucket list. With limited funds to purchase all these things, a credit card appears as a saviour. You can swiftly set up your house in a day at IKEA or any mall using your credit card. While you may intend to pay off your credit card bills the following month, you may end up spending so much that it becomes impossible, and this is where the credit card's "Minimum payable amount" feature comes into play. It may feel good only to pay Rs 6,000 instead of the total Rs 60,000. You may again plan to pay off the remaining amount the next month, and this is how you fall into the trap. Credit card companies impose very high interest rates on your unpaid bills, causing the amount owed to balloon.

If loans are considered flawed, you might wonder why wealthy individuals like Adani, Ambani, and Elon Musk take out loans worth millions and billions. Why don't they fall into a loan trap? The answer is that prominent business figures like Adani and Ambani take out loans not to buy consumer goods like phones or cars but to invest in their businesses, expand them, and generate more income. They use loaned money to create assets, while ordinary individuals use loans to create liabilities. Banks and credit card companies entice us to live like Ambani and Adani by taking out loans and selling us dreams of living a lavish lifestyle through borrowing.

It's essential never to make the mistake of taking out a loan to improve your lifestyle. This also applies to taking a loan to invest in the stock market or real estate. Wealthy individuals have a team of financial advisors to manage their finances. When they take out large loans, they carefully calculate how to use the funds to generate more income than the loan's monthly payments. Here are some specific tips regarding loans, credit cards, and investments: -

- It's essential to be cautious when considering personal loans because they often come with high interest rates, making them costly in the long run.

- When obtaining a car loan, it's advisable to keep the loan duration between four and five years. Making a significant down payment can help minimise the total loan amount.

- Instead of buying a property with a loan, consider investing the EMI into ETFs (Nifty 50) or a good mutual fund, yielding an annualised return of 12 to 15%. This can help you accumulate enough money to purchase property in the future. The historical rate of return for real estate has been approximately 10% over the last 20 years.

- When considering real estate, it's generally advisable to do so only if you intend to live in the property or if the potential rental income exceeds the monthly mortgage payment (EMI) you would be making. This ensures that the property serves a practical purpose and provides a sound financial investment.

- When you have taken out a loan that cannot cover your loan EMIs, it is important to avoid making small investments with whatever funds you have left. Prioritise using your available funds to cover your loan EMIs instead of allocating them to small investments. This approach can help you avoid financial strain and prioritise meeting your loan obligations.

- When using a credit card, it's best to reserve it for essential expenses such as monthly groceries, car fuel, and air tickets. These are necessary expenditures that can be conveniently paid using a credit card. However, it's essential to refrain from using the credit card for non-essential or leisure activities such as shopping sprees or entertainment expenses.

- Pay the total amount due on your credit card on time to avoid incurring interest charges. This practice helps maintain financial discipline and prevents unnecessary debt accumulation.

- For payments at malls and other retail outlets, it's advisable to use UPI or cash instead of a credit card whenever possible. By using alternative payment methods, you can better manage your spending and avoid the temptation of overspending with a credit card.

- Additionally, it is wise to avoid carrying credit cards to places like IKEA or other stores where impulse purchases are made. Leaving the credit card at home for non-essential outings can reduce the likelihood of making impulsive and unnecessary purchases.

- It's advisable to have two bank accounts: a salary account (income account) and an expenditure account. Transfer the calculated monthly expenditure from your salary account to your expenditure account. Link your G-pay and credit card to the expenditure account to limit your spending. The remaining money in the salary account can be saved and invested systematically by the end of the month.

- Another method is to budget for the month in advance. On receiving your salary, allocate funds for different expenses and invest the remaining balance systematically. Whichever method you choose, be mindful of your earnings and spending.

- When considering taking out a loan, it's important to remember that it's generally wise to take a loan to acquire assets rather than liabilities. An education loan can be an asset because it can enhance your skills and increase your earning capacity. Investing in education means investing in yourself and your future earning potential.

- It is essential to remember that expenditure refers to the amount of money spent on goods and services. It should always be calculated as Income minus Investment. Devoting time to planning and budgeting for your expenditures is crucial to ensuring a secure financial future. Understanding where your money goes and making informed decisions about your spending can significantly impact your financial stability and well-being.

30, 45, 60 Years Vision

As you transition into your professional life, it is crucial to approach planning with great care. This pertains not only to your career trajectory but also to your financial management. Each phase of life presents its own set of distinct challenges, emphasising the need to adapt your strategies accordingly. Like you wouldn't attempt to consume a large fish in one sitting, it's advantageous to segment your life into manageable periods based on your specific requirements. **You can organise your life into essential, critical, and optional categories**, and this concept extends beyond merely budgeting – it also involves allocating resources to each category. Thus, the initial focus should revolve around cultivating a habit of investing, growing your wealth and plan your expenditures.

When it comes to managing finances, it's essential to consider the financial journey in different stages that align with your needs and earning potential. To provide a comprehensive explanation, I will categorise these stages into three parts: -

30-Year Vision

- As you plan your 30-year vision, prioritise accumulating funds for your essential needs. Upon securing a job, setting specific financial objectives that cater to your immediate requirements is crucial, which may surface within the first 5 to 7 years. During this initial phase of your career, it's pivotal to allocate resources towards personal and financial goals, such as saving for marriage, purchasing a home, acquiring a car or bike, and more.

- The first 5 to 7 years of your professional life is a crucial period for shaping your career trajectory and addressing your personal and financial aspirations. It's of utmost importance to exercise prudence during this period, as desires often exceed available resources. By the time you reach 30, you may find yourself shouldering responsibilities towards your parents or siblings. This phase often involves aspirations for major life events such as owning a car and planning for marriage. It's common for individuals to consider various types of loans, including vehicle, personal, education, and in some cases, home loans.

- It's worth noting that during this period, some young professionals may choose to invest in real estate without fully understanding the intricacies of such investments. Often, they are lured by advice to save on taxes through home loans. Among the various desires mentioned earlier, few items stand out as vital apart from education loans or allocating funds for career development. While a bike/car may be deemed essential, marriage savings could be classified as essential or desirable given the potentially limitless financial requirements associated with weddings. Setting financial limits for marriage expenditures is advisable to ensure sustainable financial planning.

45-Year Vision

- Once you achieve your 30-year Vision, you must have targets for your 45-year Vision. This Vision (between 30 to 45 years) may include various things. Children's primary education or self up-skilling (if not done until this age) should be part of the essentials. In this time frame, family responsibilities also increase; therefore, one needs to have funds for family requirements. These requirements could be essential or desirable. Foreign holidays might be on the bucket list, but leisure trips should be kept on the desirable list. One must remember that besides an increase in desirable lists and family responsibilities, these will be the most productive years of life. A person's career progresses from middle-level to vice-president or top-level leadership positions; therefore, the right work-life balance would be required.

- In addition to work-life balance, one has to take care of personal finances during this period. Your life will take an essential shape during this time. These will be the years of career building, family, and joy. You need to be very careful in these 15 years. Try to be a very good professional and a family person.

- Don't ignore your health in these years. Build assets for yourself so that you can progress towards gaining financial freedom by the end of this period. For me, financial independence is not just about retirement. Financial independence means reaching that point where you don't have to worry about finances. Things have been sorted out to the extent that you have a financial plan for all your major life goals, i.e. children's education, their marriages, house, health, and leisure.

60-Year Vision

- As you approach age 45, having most aspects of your life in order is essential. By this time, you should have a clear understanding of your career path and how your family is developing. It's an ideal time to slow down and focus on your professional life, hobbies, health, retirement goals, and post-retirement plans.

- After 45, your health should become a top priority if it hasn't been already. Your children are likely beginning their careers, and you may have responsibilities for their marriages and caring for your parents. Careful planning and organisation are essential to ensure that everything runs smoothly.

- While planning for everything else, consider your retirement and post-retirement life and prepare for that. I've seen people retire from their jobs without a plan or with a limited plan, and I've seen them struggle a lot due to improper planning. Sometimes, people experience depression after retirement due to uncertainty and an unplanned life. Others face financial difficulties post-retirement and struggle to manage their health and medical expenses. After retiring, some individuals may face an identity crisis due to reduced income and losing their previous professional status. It is crucial to save enough money for unforeseen expenses and to develop hobbies and interests, such as playing games, painting, or music, as these can be vital in maintaining a satisfying life after retirement.

Investment and Withdrawal Plan

To kick start your career, investing 30 to 40% of your salary in Index funds/ETFs for both the long term and short term, preferably in a large-cap national index, is essential. This investment should be made consistently, with a long-term perspective in mind. Only withdraw a portion when you need money from your long-term investment. It's crucial to carefully consider and only withdraw 40 to 50% of your accumulated wealth, while the rest should remain invested in the same fund. Proper planning allows you to withdraw up to 50% of your accumulated wealth every ten years after the first 20 years of investment, providing a good cash flow for your needs. Let's illustrate this with an example.

Suppose you started investing Rs 30,000 (assuming it is 25% of your salary) at the age of 25 in Nifty 50 and received a 15% annualised rate of return.

=fv(rate,nper,pmt,[pv],[type])

=fv(15%,20,(30000x12),0,1)

= Rs 4,24,11,643

As you approach 45, you will have a substantial Rs 4,24,11,643 /-in savings. You have the power to strategically withdraw Rs 2 Crore from this amount, which can be used for your essential and desirable expenses. This leaves you with a remaining balance of Rs 2,24,11,643, which you can choose to invest as a lump sum for the next ten years. Additionally, if your salary increases significantly, you can double your monthly investment to Rs 60,000 from this point onwards, potentially accelerating your financial growth. Let's calculate the potential outcome of these decisions when you turn 55.

=fv(rate,nper,pmt,[pv],[type])

=fv(15%,10,(60000x12), 22411643,1)

= Rs 10,74,79,074

When you turn 55, you will have almost 11 Cr. You can withdraw 5 Cr from this amount and keep the rest invested without making any monthly contributions, as you will be approaching your retirement age. By turning 65, you will still have close to 24 Cr. This demonstrates the power of compounding with disciplined and planned investment. You will always have an adequate supply of money. I have not adjusted this wealth against inflation, but you will still have plenty of money even after doing so. This kind of financial security is only possible when you remain a disciplined investor and plan your life carefully rather than leaving things to chance.

Developing the habit of early and wise investment is crucial for financial success, and having a systematic withdrawal plan complements financial well-being.

No One Wants to Become Rich Slowly

Many of us share the aspiration to achieve financial success and build wealth. While there is nothing wrong with harbouring such ambitions, it's essential to cultivate the virtue of patience. Pursuing quick wealth often leads to costly mistakes. One standard error is prematurely cashing out investments to allocate funds into volatile stocks or mutual funds. It's a widespread misconception that significant results can be achieved within 2 to 3 years, but wealth accumulation often requires a longer-term perspective of around 20 years. The key lies in allowing our assets to grow through the power of compounding, which is the process where the value of an investment increases due to the interest being added to the principal over time. **It's vital to remember that time is a crucial factor in the compounding formula, as the value of money grows substantially over extended periods.**

It's crucial to remember that even a 1 to 2% increase in your rate of return can significantly impact your long-term wealth. One common mistake is investing without sufficient knowledge and relying on advice from various agents. Understanding stock market movements is not overly complex, but it's essential to be cautious in the early stages of investing. By dedicating just an hour a day to read about investment techniques, you can gain a solid understanding in a year or two. Spending time regularly to learn about personal finance can also greatly enhance your experience. Until you have a good grasp of investing, consider investing in the National index through Index Funds or ETFs. Remember that becoming wealthy through investing requires effort and commitment. It's not necessary to attend a finance college to understand investing, as there are simple tools and methods available. If you still need to figure out the stock market, continue investing in the national index, as the national large-cap index is only likely to fail if the nation faces economic bankruptcy. While even **the best stock can become worthless over time, a country cannot economically cease to exist**.

Investing without careful consideration or accidentally is the worst way to lose money. The first step before investing is budgeting. Mindful budgeting and intelligent investing are crucial for building wealth, and they work together. When we want to buy a mobile phone, we do lots of research, compare features, go through 'you tube' reviews and consider value for money, but when it comes to investing, we often pay limited attention. We must devote time and consideration to investing, just as before buying a mobile phone. Creating a stable financial future is quite simple, as long as you have a clear vision and desire. Investing should not be just an option on your to-do list; it should be your life's top priority. Even insects, birds, and animals save food for rainy days. If these creatures can understand the importance of securing their future by investing or saving some resources for difficult times, why can't we, as human beings, do the same?

The teachings in this chapter are aimed at creating wealth. Since I am targeting young professionals like you, I haven't delved into direct stock investing or selecting mutual funds in detail. Discussing these topics could be risky as it may distract you from your career. My goal is to provide you with a simple yet effective method for building wealth in the early years of your job. By following a disciplined approach to investing, you will naturally learn more advanced techniques over time. Start small and take gradual steps to grow your money, and things will eventually fall into place. Making mistakes with your investments is normal, but don't worry; learn from them and keep investing. Many young professionals either overspend or invest without understanding the ins and outs of investing.

Investing in individual stocks involves a lot of research and carries risks. I've realised that not all stocks in a portfolio yield positive returns. Some consistently result in negative returns, making it challenging to achieve more than an 18% to 20% Compound Annual Growth Rate (CAGR) in the long term. Expecting more than a 25% CAGR would be akin to gambling.

That's why I prefer Index funds or Exchange-Traded Funds (ETFs), such as the Nifty 50, gold, midcap, or Nifty IT. This type of investment is straightforward and akin to a Fixed Deposit (FD) investment, with the caveat that returns may be negative for a certain period during bearish stock markets, especially for short investment horizons. However, there's nothing to worry about for long-term investments (say, over ten years). Economies with solid growth eventually recover from short-term downturns.

It's essential to understand that stock market movements are cyclical, with bearish and bullish phases. The key is identifying opportunities in a bearish market and taking profits in a bullish market while staying invested. **Remember, compounding is often called the world's eighth wonder, and giving your money time to grow is crucial.** Disciplined investing, starting early in one's professional career, is essential. Even if the amount to be invested is small, it's crucial to continue investing monthly and year after year.

Therefore, one must have sufficient patience in the process of accumulating wealth. Wealth creation is not solely about income; it depends on saving and investment. Money requires time and discipline to grow.

Takeaways from Chapter-2

- Earning and spending are both crucial, but the skill of spending money wisely holds greater significance in the journey towards wealth creation.

- Money plays a vital role in our lives. It is necessary not just for survival but also for pursuing passions and making meaningful contributions to society.

- Don't let others' opinions dictate your financial choices. It is essential to make decisions based on your values, goals, and circumstances.

- When investing and growing your money, it's crucial to consider options that outpace inflation and yield a positive return.

- The stock market can be complex and unpredictable, making it a daunting choice for many individuals. Before entering the stock market for investing in stocks directly, it's essential to thoroughly understand its dynamics and the many factors that drive its fluctuations.

- When investing in the stock market, exploring exchange-traded funds (ETFs) or index funds is recommended, as they provide better and less volatile results than individual stock picking.

- ETFs and index funds are often less influenced by the performance of individual companies, which can contribute to more stable and predictable returns over the long term.

- Fixed Deposits (FDs) are a reliable option for temporary money parking. They offer a secure way to earn interest on your savings while keeping your funds accessible.

- When considering real estate investments, it's prudent to explore commercial properties. Compared to investing in multiple residential properties such as houses or flats, commercial properties have the potential to yield higher rental income and offer better overall growth returns.

- Conduct thorough research and seek professional advice before making real estate investment decisions.
- When considering using a loan to purchase plots, it is essential to thoroughly analyse the project's potential for growth. This includes calculating the rate of return and interest rate to ensure an informed decision.
- Instead of direct real estate investment, one may want to explore the promising options of Index Funds or Exchange-Traded Funds (ETFs). These investment vehicles offer the potential for higher returns and greater liquidity over the long term.
- Index funds and ETFs, in particular, are favored for their simplicity, low cost, and diversification benefits, which can instill a sense of optimism in your investment choices.
- In the realm of mutual funds, it's worth noting that past winners may not always maintain their position.
- Patience, consistency, and discipline are essential in building wealth. Financial goals should be clearly defined across short-term (30-year), mid-term (45-year), and long-term (60-year) time horizons.
- To manage finances effectively, consider maintaining two bank accounts: a salary account to receive income and an expenditure account for monthly spending.
- By transferring the calculated monthly expenditure from the salary account to the expenditure account and linking services like G-pay and credit cards to the expenditure account, you can effectively control and limit your spending while systematically saving and investing the remaining funds by month-end.

- One must recognise that time plays a pivotal role in the compounding formula, as the value of money grows significantly over extended periods.

- It is crucial to understand that a stock with outstanding potential can diminish in value over time; however, a country's entire economy will not. Therefore, prioritising long-term investments and exercising patience are crucial to sustainable financial growth.

CHAPTER 3

FINDING SENORITA OR SENOR

Marriage: Is it a Love Affair or a Management

Marriage is a significant and cherished milestone in everybody's life. A successful marriage has the potential to amplify life's joy and contribute to overall success. It extends beyond reproduction and embraces the journey of companionship, bonding, support, love, and care. Choosing a life partner is one of the most crucial decisions in life and should be approached with great thought and mindfulness. **There's a popular notion that finding a compatible life partner is more intricate than securing a good job** and I believe this to be true.

Marriage can be a source of both joy and frustration for many people. Marital discord is common, and differences between partners are expected due to the union of two distinct individuals. Even marrying a close friend does not guarantee a smooth ride, as individuals have different backgrounds, needs, and desires. Common reasons for marital problems include lack of communication, intimacy, understanding, financial issues, and the most importantly differing expectations. The specific reasons for a troubled marriage vary from couple to couple.

Many people enter into marriage without giving it much thought. Getting married simply because it's expected at a certain age or due to biological urges should not be the sole basis for marriage. The decision to get married should be based not only on societal and physical needs but also on the level of commitment and, most importantly, the willingness to share life with someone. An individual must have a clear mindset before deciding to get married.

When making important decisions, such as buying our first phone, car or home; we often spend a lot of time researching and seeking advice from family and friends. However, the decision to get married requires even more careful consideration than purchasing an item. Many people feel pressured into marriage by family or follow their instincts without much thought, leading to problems. Marriage is a lifelong commitment that involves the union of two individuals at physical, mental, and emotional levels. It's important to be ready to care for another person in addition to oneself. Marriage is more than living together under one roof; it requires love, compassion, and commitment. Marriage is about managing a relationship with these essential elements, and if they are present, it can lead to a successful and fulfilling partnership.

Marriage is often seen as a loving relationship involving care, intimacy, and affection. However, effective management is required to maintain these elements. Successful management necessitates a sincere approach, dedication, selflessness, and sharing. It involves stepping out of one's comfort zone. Crucially, **understanding and support are essential** for successful marriage management. This means understanding each other's needs and desires and supporting each other in fulfilling them. Unfortunately, many couples impose their will and desires on each other instead of offering support.

Additionally, they often expect their partners to understand them first rather than trying to understand each other. This leads to a competition where love, compassion, care, and respect are often lost. Many couples embark on a mission to improve their partner post-marriage, essentially treating it as an improvisation project. They begin teaching each other how to sleep, walk, eat, drink, and manage themselves. They get engrossed so much so that they forget they are not living in a halfway house or reformatory

(Sudhar grah). They are still in marriage where love, compassion and care are more important than improvisation drive.

A Significant Decision

Certain things must be kept in mind before finding or deciding on a match, whether someone is looking for Senorita or Senor. As I mentioned earlier, marriage is a union of two individuals, and these two individuals may come from different families and cultures or may be from different castes or religions. While as friends, we don't face much problem accepting these differences, it matters a lot when it is a matter of sharing life (not only bed).

Two individuals who were good friends in college and used to share a strong bond may become an unsuccessful married couple due to their different priorities and habits in life. One person may be very laid-back in their personal life but very ambitious professionally. On the other hand, their partner may have obsessive-compulsive disorder (OCD) or maybe someone who likes to manage their personal life well and has a relaxed attitude towards their professional life. One might be focused on chasing money and luxuries, while the other prioritises companionship and family. Couples may have many contrasting habits, and these differences are likely due to their different upbringings and personal natures. Sometimes, these personal habits are so entrenched that no one wants to compromise or change, let alone change themselves. Generally, couples try to change their partner's habits to align with their own instead of aligning with their partner's habits.

It's important to remember that people's priorities change as they age. For instance, men often focus on their careers in their 30s and 40s rather than spending time with their families. Meanwhile, women tend to prioritise their children over their jobs or husbands during this stage of life. While this isn't always the case, **it's common for men and women to shift their priorities as they age.** This is why childhood friends may behave differently as spouses than in college.

Couples often try to impose their will or habits on their partners and expect them to change. They put all their effort into trying to improve their partner rather than accepting them the way they are, which causes conflict in the relationship. On the other hand, if these individuals focus on giving each other space instead of trying to change each other, there is a greater chance of peace.

Hence, choosing Senorita or Senor should be approached with careful consideration and mindfulness. It should be a well-considered decision rather than an impulsive or emotionally driven one. Selecting a life partner is a significant decision that can impact an individual's life positively or negatively. While there is no foolproof formula for choosing a life partner, certain fundamental aspects should be considered when contemplating marriage. The criteria for selecting a life partner will vary from person to person based on individual needs and desires.

Upbringing and Our Surroundings

In ancient times, our ancestors greatly emphasised marrying within the same social status, caste, creed, and religion. For example, kings would only marry their daughters to other kings. Society was divided into different castes based on people's professions, and individuals were also segregated based on religious beliefs. Due to these factors, people preferred to marry within the same or similar social groups. A child was believed to inherit qualities from their parents based on their profession and religious beliefs. For example, it was thought that a warrior's child would possess warrior-like attributes, and a clergy's child would exhibit qualities similar to those of clergy. This belief stemmed from the idea that children inherit genes or habits from their parents and from the environment in which they are bought up.

As society expanded and became more liberal, the acceptance of inter-caste, inter-religious, and inter-regional marriages also grew. I personally don't see any issue with inter-caste, inter-religion, or inter-regional marriages. The caste system was initially based on an individual's occupation, and I believe that all human beings are equal and should be treated with equal importance and rights. However, I have realised that a child's upbringing and personality development are often influenced by the society or environment in which they are raised. A child's personality development also depends upon the nature of parents' profession. For example, life in the armed forces creates a unique and close-knit culture, different from civilian society. This lifestyle affects not only the personnel but also their families. Living in military stations exposes individuals to a different way of life, and frequent relocations lead to an openness to accepting other cultures and habits. Children in military families become accustomed to making new friends at each new station, fostering a liberal attitude towards different castes, creeds, religions, and regions. Life within military stations is distinctly different from life outside of military stations.

Similarly, the upbringing and life experiences of a child of an engineer, doctor, politician, or diplomat would be different. Our upbringing shapes our outlook, and individuals are conditioned differently based on their birthplace and upbringing. A person born into a Brahmin (clergy) family is more likely to have a religious (ritualistic) outlook, while a Marwari child is often conditioned to have business traits. A Jewish child might be conditioned to perceive a Muslim or Christian as different, if not as an enemy. Similarly, children born in Pakistan are often conditioned to view India as an enemy rather than as a friend. Our birthplace and upbringing play a significant role in shaping our personalities.

A person from Bihar state will die for Sattu and Litti-chokha (their staple food), and on the other hand, a person from Tamilnadu (or any south Indian state) may not find any taste in Litti-chokha and may be looking for their staple food Idli, Dosa, or Uttapam. A south Indian person would love to relish Idli or Dosa, even in the United States. On the same lines, a day scholar will have different personality traits than a hostler. **Our brain and body muscles get conditioned to what we have seen, tasted or gone through since childhood. Our muscle memory gets conditioned accordingly.** Our taste buds relish the type of food our mother used to make and provide us. No rich or poor may say that he does not like the food prepared by his mother.

I have noticed that our upbringing shapes specific habits within us, which become so ingrained in our lives that some of us struggle to accept anything different. I'm not trying to label anyone as good or bad, but I am saying that different environments make us different people. The upbringing and habits of a person from a salaried family will differ from those of a person from a business-oriented family. Their mindsets will be different on many levels. They will have different perspectives about money and life in general. A person who has faced challenges before achieving success will be different from someone who has always been comfortable and has never encountered hardships.

Some families have a tradition or culture of removing footwear before entering the house, but this is not the case in many other families. Some families are pure vegetarians; however, in other families, any type of food is acceptable. Some families are orthodox and traditional, while others have more liberal mindsets. These minor differences in family traditions, upbringing, and values can sometimes lead to conflicts after marriage.

The differences in our upbringing and the status of our family members create two levels of distinction. Whether we acknowledge it or not, our immediate family members' varying levels of education and financial stability significantly impact our lives. The acceptance level of family members is often influenced by their educational background, financial situation, and life experiences.

We all understand these differences, but after marriage, we often want our partner and their family members to change rather than we change ourselves. For example, if I am not used to removing my shoes before entering the house, I might expect my partner to change her habits instead of me learning to remove my shoes. Even slight differences like this can cause problems in married life. I've seen many people argue over minor issues, which has negatively impacted their lives.

A person's managerial skills are crucial when it comes to handling differences. We can significantly improve our lives by giving each other space and effectively managing these differences. It's important not to expect others to change their habits which they possess since their childhood. And if change is necessary, let's allow a reasonable amount of time for it to happen.

Often, we accept differences reluctantly and forcefully, only acknowledging the differences and not the person. Only a few of us are open to discussing differences and are willing to work on accepting or improving them. Sometimes, when I observe particular couples, they seem destined to make each other's life miserable. They seem to be out for each other's blood, living as if they are doing a favour by sharing their lives with their partners.

Suppose both individuals in a marriage are sensible and have compassion, love, care, and respect for each other. In that case, I don't think they will face any problems in their married life, regardless of caste, creed, religion, or region. In such cases, adjustments happen automatically due to understanding each other's emotions. Spiritual guru Sadhguru has beautifully said, **"Once your relationships are about sharing your joy, rather than extracting joy out of someone else, you can have wonderful relationships with anyone."**

Upbringing and surroundings continue to shape individuals differently, leading to varying opinions, needs, and desires. Therefore, it's essential to base marriage on respect, trust, care, and understanding or to develop exceptional managerial skills to navigate expectations without conflict. A marriage built on respect, trust, care, and understanding will be long-lasting, while one built on expectations will be short-lived.

Are We Hard-Wired

Until a few decades ago, people typically stayed close to their roots and didn't venture far from their native places. Their lives revolved around their native rituals, environment, and culture. However, as people started relocating for work or education, they began to experience and embrace new cultures and traditions. This exposure led to more open-mindedness and influenced their eating and living habits.

Exposure to different cultures, traditions, cuisines, weather, and places can broaden our minds and make us more open, accepting, and generous. While individuals may remain attached to their customs, their acceptance for others can change. Openness doesn't completely change people, as it's challenging to alter basic instincts, but it does make individuals more open-minded. For example, when people from South India travel to North India, they may face difficulties with language, food, and attire. However, their acceptance of these differences improves as they start living in North India. The same is true vice-versa.

In the beginning, married life seems perfect due to physical intimacy. However, after a few months, people begin to notice different habits in their partners and often try to change their partners' habits instead of accepting them as they are or changing themselves. Exposure to the world can change a person's outlook, and the same applies to marriages. When individuals have an open mind and accept everything in its natural form, language, caste, creed, culture, and religion, differences can vanish. We do not remain hard-wired when we are exposed to the world. We can change or update our mindset with time and different places. We feel happy to explore new things and remain open to accepting new and different things without seeing them as taboo.

I have an example to share. I used to be primarily vegetarian until I was in 12th grade. Occasionally, I would eat eggs. When I moved to a bigger city for higher studies, I started eating chicken casually in the company of my friends. Later, when I joined the armed forces and moved from one place to another, I also started eating fish. So, my acceptance of non-vegetarian food and non-vegetarian people increased over time. I didn't feel awkward in non-vegetarians' company, and I began enjoying their company. There are extreme examples, too, where a hardcore non-vegetarian has turned into a vegan in the company of newly made friends. Exposure to the outer world opens you up to multiple opportunities. Nothing is inherently good or bad. One should not become judgmental about others just because of their habits. If you like a potato, that's your choice; if some people like chicken, that's their choice. Accepting people the way they are makes you a better and big-hearted person and you will likely have less pressure and problem in dealing with new people.

The change in outlook that comes with exposure is not guaranteed and gospel. I have witnessed individuals who remain just as inflexible and closed-minded as they were in their youth despite being exposed to various experiences. Some people are so entrenched in their beliefs that they are unwilling to accept others. They may feign openness and generosity, but their true nature becomes evident after a few interactions or when you start living with them. Such individuals may be encountered not only in marriages but also in workplaces. Regardless of the knowledge they acquire, they remain unchanged. These people cannot break free from their fundamental character and only undergo a superficial transformation through exposure to the outside world. As you spend more time with them, their facade diminishes, revealing their true nature. Sometimes, their deep-seated roots prevent them from changing, and even if they attempt to do so, their parents or relatives hinder their progress, instilling a fear of social ostracism. They lack the ability to influence their parents or others within their community. While they may embrace different cultures and customs individually, within their community or society, they prefer to remain connected to their roots and adhere to all the customs and traditions. These individuals maintain a rebellious or extremist stance throughout their lives and will always seek to change their partners by the customs and traditions of their community. Dealing with such individuals after marriage is challenging, as they tend to impose their will on their spouse.

Regional influence, customs, traditions, rituals, and language can challenge a happy married life. To succeed in marriage, individuals should be open-hearted, broad-minded, and having capability to deeply understand and accept their spouse. A marriage can thrive despite differences if there is mutual respect and acceptance. Mutual respect cannot exist without acknowledging each other as we are, without conditions or prejudices. It's important not to try to change the other person but to accept them as they are.

We all change as we grow older, encounter new challenges, and accumulate new experiences, providing us with hope for a better life. Therefore, in the early stages of marriage, we must provide our spouses with the time and space to adjust to the new intricacies of married life.

Habits, Likes and Dislikes

Regional customs, traditions, religion, and rituals influence our habits and preferences, impacting our personalities and thought processes. If not handled carefully, these factors can create rifts in relationships. We tend to believe in our customs and traditions, making it difficult to accept other religions easily due to our upbringing. While many may appear accepting of different religions when speaking to others, their personal beliefs may differ. This contradiction between preaching and practice is common.

Even small habits like getting up early, doing evening prayers, or keeping a religious fast may irritate one's partner in a marriage. Some people are early to bed and early to rise; some want a cup of tea first thing in the morning, and some may like to work out; some might be too lazy to get out of bed for any physical activity, and some might prefer outdoor activities; some like to remain glued to the TV, and some enjoy reading books; some love to talk and some are more serious; some are creative, and some prefer to enjoy their life in shopping malls. The key to success in all such cases is accepting each other the way they are. Even with so many differences, one must look for commonalities, or both partners must try to enjoy each other's habits. Sometimes, even taking a small positive step may bring happiness to married life. In a marriage, likes and dislikes should not be imposed on each other; they should be respected and accepted to create adequate space to minimise friction.

Responsibilities and Expectations

Married life is a serious commitment. Both partners are responsible for their own lives and must share equal responsibility for their partner's well-being. Marriages are meant to fulfill social, biological, and emotional needs. It's important to remember that being married requires effort from both partners to succeed. Your actions not only affect your own life but also impact your partner's. In a marriage, there are expectations for understanding, support, cooperation, creativity, hard work, and love. Recognising that your partner also expects the same from you is essential. Every partner wants a happy, healthy, wealthy, comfortable, and loving life. Problems arise when expectations overshadow responsibilities. Expectations, by nature, can be selfish and can lead to desiring things without considering others. However, taking responsibility means putting in the effort to make things work. Often, marriages suffer when expectations take precedence over responsibility and accountability.

In the past, roles and responsibilities within a marriage were well-defined. Men were typically seen as the breadwinners, responsible for earning money to support the family, while women were primarily responsible for household chores and childcare. Men generally had fewer responsibilities when it came to caring for the home or children, while women's roles focused on caring for the household and the children.

The traditional division of responsibilities between men and women has evolved. Both partners now work and share household and marital duties. In today's world, where nuclear families are common, there is a greater need for shared responsibilities compared to the past when joint families were prevalent. In a joint family setup, young couples often rely on the support of family members to start their own families. This support becomes even more crucial when both partners are working. When a new baby arrives, parental support is essential for childcare and learning effective parenting techniques. Older family members play a vital role in instilling good habits in children. It's not just adults who need companionship; children also benefit from the presence of older family members. Improper care, such as relying solely on maids or daycare centers, can negatively impact a child's growth, leading to malnutrition or stunted development. Unlike maids, grandparents provide essential care, love, affection, and moral guidance through storytelling and nurturing.

Young couples often experience anxiety and stress due to the added responsibilities of raising their children. Raising a child demands full-time attention and cannot be completely outsourced. The arrival of a new family member can lead to turbulence in young marriages. Therefore, it's crucial to marry someone who understands and shares responsibilities. Marriage is not just about staying together in an intimate relationship; it's about sharing mutual responsibility. If one person earns, the other should contribute to household tasks. While services like Zomato and Swiggy can provide meals, they can't replace the need for a functional kitchen.

Similarly, a couple cannot rely solely on hotels for shelter. Unless they are exceptionally affluent, both partners should be actively involved in household chores. This not only lightens the load but also fosters a sense of shared responsibility, a cornerstone of a harmonious marriage.

Maids cannot be the housekeeping managers of your house and can carry the responsibility of arranging the home properly.

A married couple has to involve themselves in the household chores. Yes, if you are filthy rich like certain film stars, advocates and people in business, then you can outsource the management of your house to a management team. Both partners should share equal responsibility in managing the home, as traditional gender roles have blurred. It's essential to share responsibilities to live happily in marriage.

The demarcation of responsibilities of men and women has blurred now, so both of them should know the work of each

other's domain. When women can share responsibilities in earning bread for the home, men should also help raise children and do household chores. We must share duties in managing things as we do with our hostel roommates. Sometimes, it is better to remain roommates in a married life so that we can learn to give space to each other and share responsibilities. To live happily married, we must learn to share house responsibilities. Otherwise, we would only expect our counterparts to do things, and slowly, we would create rifts in the relationship. **Sharing responsibilities is one of the most essential parts of married life.**

Finding a Life Partner

By now, you must have understood that marriage is a complex subject. Let me summarise what I have said so far.

- Marriage is a management process with love, compassion, and commitment ingredients. Once you have selected your partner, understand and accept her/ him as they are.

- Declare before marriage if you have any strong like or dislike. You have to loudly declare it before marriage, and after marriage, avoid forcing things.

- Upbringing and the environment in which a person has been brought up make a difference. Exposure to the world brings openness and increases acceptance.

- Different habits create distinct personalities. It would be the best to be responsible for your partner's life, and both partners should be responsible for managing married life and family.

- In marriage, learn to give space to each other and try to be just roommates as far as space sharing is concerned. Enjoy togetherness rather imposing things.

- Don't take your partner for granted or turn deaf/ blind towards needs and desires of your partner. If you turn deaf/ blind, marriage will derail.
- A true relationship is about sharing emotions, love, joy and companionship.

Uff... so much complexity (ha ha ha), and we think marriage is a game. Big, fat Indian weddings with lots of dance, music, and food are not a guarantee for a happy married life. I aim not to scare you but to make you aware of marriage requirements. I can assure you that if you understand and work on these requirements, you can have a wonderful life. Though nothing is guaranteed, the probability of a successful married life is very high if the decision to marry is conscious and not a knee-jerk reaction. Here are a few tips that may help you in your decision-making for marriage.

It is often advisable to seek a partner from a similar background. When upbringing is identical, there is a higher likelihood of sharing similar thought processes. While this is not a strict rule, it can increase the probability of a successful relationship. Ultimately, marriage is about sharing life with someone for the long term. Similar upbringing can lead to more commonalities, such as shared family traditions, customs, and rituals. Having common ground can also make it easier to be accepted by each other's families. As humans, we tend to resist change and prefer to stay within our comfort zones. Only a few people are willing to change their habits because of new family members. Some may try to adapt after marriage, but many give up quickly, leading to friction. Different families may have varying daily routines, such as waking up times, morning rituals, eating habits, and outlooks on life. Having commonalities can help smooth the transition into a new life after marriage.

Consider finding a partner with a similar professional background or professional lifestyle. Different professions have different demands, such as extensive travel, irregular working hours, heavy reading, or standard 9-to-5 routines. These demands can lead to developing different habits, which may cause friction if not appropriately managed. In many cases, couples attempt to change their partners or seek compromises. Similar professions can help to alleviate differences that may cause friction in daily life. However, one drawback of having similar professions is the potential for competition between partners, which can lead to negative feelings or a desire to outdo one another. Couples need to guard against this and remember that they are a team. Supporting each other's professional growth can lead to greater happiness, like how we help our friends by sharing our knowledge during exams.

Even when people share similar backgrounds and professions, their life partners are not guaranteed to be just like them. There may be many personality differences, which can cause friction in married life. It's challenging to change an adult's personality. People's personalities change only when they realise what is good or bad for them. Some individuals are staunch non-vegetarians, smokers, or alcohol drinkers, and no amount of persuasion can change them unless they realise the need to change for themselves. Sometimes, we have moments of self-realisation and we improve ourselves. Other times, our friends or professional environment can influence our lives. Generally, we change in some way every ten years through self-realisation or various life events. The best way to deal with such friction is to accept things as they are. It's easier said than done, but often there are no better options. Each of us is responsible for our own lives, and sooner or later, we may realise the kind of life we live. Not everyone has the power or self-control to overcome their weaknesses, so we should accept things as they are when we can't do much about them. Acceptance is a virtue; it gives you the strength to look beyond. In a marriage, we should never force our ways on our partners. We can always encourage them to adopt certain behaviours, but we should limit our influence to suggestions or encouragement; we should never try to impose our ways to bring about changes.

We must understand the reasons why we got married. As social creatures, we find joy in the company of others when it involves sharing happiness. We seek happiness, often pursuing it through money, career success, and material possessions. A fulfilling marriage can provide long-term happiness and reduce the need for worldly pursuits. It's essential to comprehend the dynamics of married life and the role of a life partner. In marriage and life, learning to accept differences gracefully is crucial. Varying opinions and habits are natural, as no two individuals are alike. Embracing these differences and sharing joy are the keys to a happy married life. It will be challenging to navigate married life if we resist change.

Exposure to different things can make you more open-minded and broaden your horizons. Increased exposure can lead to greater acceptance of other cultures and traditions. A better education can make you better by changing your perception of different things. Therefore, if your life partner has been exposed to various aspects of life, they may be more accommodating, even with different habits. This is why the exposure factor may be critical in choosing a life partner.

My next point is for you: Before considering marriage, be clear in your mind that you are going to take care of another life besides your own. Marriage comes with many responsibilities for both partners, and you must realise that you cannot expect the other person to be more responsible than you are. Responsibility starts with you. If you are ready to take care of another life alongside your own, consider the points I discussed earlier. If not, take your time, understand your professional and personal commitments, and decide. Finding your partner should be a well-thought-out and conscious decision, not based on any compulsion.

Last but not least, no relationship can be sustained for long without love and respect. Love and respect must be mutual and not demanded from others. One should not wait to give love and respect only to receive the same. Please do not measure love and respect before giving them. They should come willingly and thoughtfully.

Remember, no relationship always runs smoothly. Relationships with human beings (I am not talking about robots) are filled with selflessness, selfishness, love, hate, respect, arguments, misunderstandings, and emotions. Handling all types of relationships requires the utmost care.

Whatever I discussed about marriage will help you find your Senorita now, and I am sure you will lead a wonderful married life.

Takeaways from Chapter-3

- Marriage is often perceived as a deep, affectionate bond requiring ongoing attention and nurturing. The key to a fulfilling marital relationship is effective management with sustains care, intimacy, and compassion.

- Successful marriage management requires an earnest and dedicated approach, selflessness, and a willingness to share. It involves stepping out of one's comfort zone and making decisions based on personal values rather than being swayed by the opinions of others.

- As individuals mature, their priorities often shift, with both men and women experiencing changes in their perspectives and goals.

- Our upbringing plays a significant role in shaping our behaviours and habits, which can become deeply ingrained in our lives and influence how we perceive and respond to various situations.

- Our brain and body muscles are conditioned by our experiences, tastes, and what we've been exposed to since childhood. These experiences shape our muscle memory, leading to ingrained responses and behaviours. Recognising and understanding these patterns is the key to effective relationship management.

- When it comes to managing differences in a relationship, the ability to communicate effectively and respect each other's individuality is crucial.

- **In healthy relationships, the focus should be on companionship rather than imposing will on the partner**. This perspective can lead to fulfilling connections with all kinds of people.

- Regional influences, customs, traditions, rituals, and language differences can challenge a happy married life. It's essential to recognise the impact of these elements and navigate them together as a couple.

- Marriage requires a serious commitment from both partners. Each person is responsible for their well-being and must share equal responsibility for their partner's well-being.

- As traditional gender roles evolve, both partners must understand and appreciate each other's contributions. The division of responsibilities between men and women has become less rigid, so both partners need to know each other's domains.

- Marriage can be akin to a management process, requiring love, compassion, and commitment as essential ingredients. Once a partner has been chosen, it's crucial to fully understand and accept them for who they are.

- This acceptance and understanding lay the foundation for a successful and enduring partnership.

CHAPTER 4

ADDITIONAL CHAPTER
21 Jul 23/ 2010 hr

I hadn't planned to write this chapter, but a recent incident compelled me. Yesterday, your mother informed me that a second-semester student from your college had taken his own life, possibly due to being scolded by a teacher (exact reason not yet known). This news has deeply saddened me, and my heart goes out to the family and friends of the student. It's challenging to comprehend the loss of someone's child. Such incidents are genuinely heartbreaking for the parents. I don't want to speculate on the reasons behind this tragic decision. Only the person who is no longer with us knows the exact reasons. Unfortunately, this is not an isolated case, as there have been numerous instances of young scholars and even young air warriors taking such extreme steps.

In this chapter, I will write with total respect and dignity for all those who have ended their lives for whatever reasons. It is not easy to end your own life. When someone decides to end his life, he does so due to multiple pressures and psychological conditions created by his surroundings. Each one of us wants to live happily and do lots of good work. Everyone on this planet wants recognition, success, and financial stability. No one wants to live a miserable life.

Suicide is a complex subject, and I understand that life is also complex. We face difficult situations at every stage of life. At times, things do not happen according to our wishes or convenience. Life events can become frustrating when our expectations are not fulfilled. However, taking one's own life is not the solution. The solution to life's difficulties lies in facing them with courage and conviction.

When children are very young, one year old or so, they struggle even to walk but they continue trying even after repeated failures. They do not try to end their lives just because they can't walk. Have you ever seen birds and animals struggling to survive in the presence of bigger, stronger, and deadlier animals and choosing to end their lives? No bird or animal commits suicide due to life's difficulties.

Feeling of Dejection

I have encountered many challenging situations in life that can lead to feelings of melancholy or sadness. This psychological pressure can be so intense that individuals may consider ending their lives. However, it's essential to understand that no situation should ever become a reason to end one's life.

I've observed that students often experience sadness or frustration at some point due to study pressures, competition, peer pressure, or family expectations. Similarly, bad marriages can make one feel trapped and gloomy. Another common scenario is when parents of marriageable children struggle to find suitable matches for social or financial reasons. Parents may also feel dejected when their children engage in antisocial behaviour or become rebellious, leading to social isolation and depression.

Furthermore, parents who have dedicated their lives to their children may feel neglected or abandoned once their children are settled and fail to care for them. Additionally, the untimely death of a close family member, such as a spouse or young child, can bring about feelings of sadness and despair. Numerous phases in life can lead to feelings of melancholy and sorrow, but it's essential to learn how to cope with each situation.

It's crucial to remember that the feeling of dejection is temporary. We need to remain calm and wait for the situation to improve. Decisions about life events should not be made impulsively. Before making any decision, whether good or bad, we need to carefully consider the decision and its potential consequences.

I want you to understand life in its true sense. First, we must know that nothing is more significant than living a life; everything else is secondary. Success and failures are part of life. We need to look beyond success and failures. Success and failures are just some of the stoppages in our journey of life and not the complete life. We should not feel too happy about success and should not feel sad about failures. Life has to move on. Everyone is learning the reasons for their existence. Each one of us goes through happy and frustrating moments. One needs to explore oneself until one can make a difference in his or somebody else's life.

Each of us is supposed to do our part and keep exploring life. We don't need to look at life in a straight line. **Life is more like a zigzag line, so if we don't have clarity of thoughts, let's not focus too far ahead. Just focus on the next turn and do well**. Let's not get weighed down by uncertainties after the turn. We need to focus on the process rather than on the result. When we start focusing on the result, we put pressure on ourselves and fear failure. Instead, we should focus on the process to enjoy the journey and not worry about the results. A student should prioritise understanding subjects and their practical use over focusing on grades. A professional should prioritise hard work and sincerity, with results following naturally. We must look at living life in whatever role we are in rather than looking too far.

Social Pressure

We are social animals and take things very seriously when something happens to us publicly. Whether it is an insult or praise, it touches our hearts. We take social insult or praise as disapproval or approval of society on that particular issue. We feel glad if we are socially praised for our actions. For instance, when we achieve good grades or get promoted and are praised or lauded by family and friends, we celebrate by throwing parties or distributing sweets.

Conversely, if we fail to get a promotion or perform poorly in a class, our biggest fear is societal judgment. We fear rejection and mockery as we fail to prove our potential. It's important to understand that society is made up of people like us. No one has come from heaven to form society. Everyone in society is fearful of the same fear of rejection. As I mentioned, one must learn the art of losing gracefully. If we accept our mistakes rather than justifying them and accept our defeats rather than making excuses for our failures, no one can reject or insult us. We must develop wisdom to identify our strengths and limitations. We must develop the courage to accept our limitations.

Look at the losing team's captain at the post-match ceremony. If the captain accepts defeat gracefully and analyses the reasons for the loss, no one will criticise him. However, he will be criticised sooner or later if he tries to blame others or make excuses. Accepting your own mistake and defeat gracefully is one of the greatest virtues. Those unable to develop this quality may feel humiliated and even take extreme steps as they cannot handle the humiliation.

My philosophy on failures is simple: accept them and move on. One or two failures should not be a reason to give up on life; even a hundred failures should not deter us from moving forward. After facing failures, it's essential to keep pushing, stay composed, maintain a sense of calm and collectedness, analyse the situation, and come back with some form of success. Most of us don't achieve success on the first try; many of us succeed after multiple attempts. Have you ever observed an ant climbing a wall with a sugar ball in its mouth? It may fail numerous times but gets back up and starts climbing again. It doesn't lose heart and give up on its efforts. It remains focused, sincere, and works hard.

Another example is the 'Hit Me doll' that gets up every time after each punch. Make yourself tough enough to face failures with a smile like the 'Hit Me doll'. Instead of feeling ashamed of your failures, learn lessons and become stronger. If you are strong enough to accept your defeat and failures, no one can put a dent in your image. Failures are like dust on your shirt; shake your body, throw away the dust, and move on. Yes, failures may delay the process of achieving success, but they cannot stop the process unless the person gives up.

Definite parameters do not define success and failure. What may cause extreme joy for one person can be seen as a disappointment by another. People set their own goals in life, and based on these goals, they measure success and failure. Each individual has to establish rules for the game of life, considering their strengths and weaknesses. Understanding and acknowledging our limitations is essential, as everyone has different capabilities and circumstances. Comparing our achievements and failures with those of others is not productive. Instead, we should focus on hard work, sincerity, and continuous learning without being overly concerned about the outcome. We must embrace all results with happiness, as they provide motivation and valuable learning experiences.

Social Perception

Society defines what is right and wrong. Many things are simply perceptions of the people around us. At times, we base our life decisions on someone else's perception. If you become more accepting of the things around you, your perception of many things will change, and you won't feel judgmental and dejected. Instead of being judgmental, be positive and take things as they come. I believe what goes against the country's laws should be unacceptable and avoided, rest other things are based on perception. It's better to acknowledge one's faults, apologise, and move on, even if one has made a mistake. Mistakes are a part of life and will continue to happen as long as we are alive. Apologising for your mistakes is not a crime; I consider it an act of bravery. It stops the argument or discussion immediately.

Expectations and Comparisons

It's natural to have expectations in life, whether they come from family, friends, or from ourselves. However, it's essential to consider these expectations realistically. Each person is unique, and comparisons and excessive expectations should be avoided. Success and failure are temporary, as life has ups and downs. Winners do not always stay on top, and losers can succeed with hard work and perseverance. Therefore, taking success and failures with a pinch of salt is essential.

It's important not to compare ourselves to others or set unrealistic expectations for ourselves. Instead, we should assess our capabilities and pursue our interests. Parents should guide their children rather than pressure them to fulfill their desires or expectations. It's crucial to allow our children to pursue their interests, even if they differ from ours. While it's natural for parents to want their children to excel in a particular field, it's essential to consider the child's inclinations and interests. This is especially relevant when a child is about to choose their higher education or career path. Sometimes, parents may project their unfulfilled dreams onto their children, pushing them in a direction that doesn't align with their true interests and capabilities. This can create unnecessary pressure on the child and reduce their chances of success. When it comes to higher education, parents and children need to explore a wide range of academic paths. They should consider each option's specific curriculum and career opportunities, aligning these with the child's interests and inclinations. This approach ensures that individual passion drives educational decisions rather than popular trends or social expectations. Parents must start this process just after schooling, and if needed, they must seek professional help in deciding their child's future.

Wrong Assessment of Own Capabilities

Sometimes, we make incorrect assessments of our capabilities. We may either underestimate or overestimate ourselves. Parents or experienced individuals should assist children in understanding their abilities. Children should not be pressured into pursuing paths that do not align with their interests. It is also the child's responsibility to understand their capabilities and discuss them with their parents.

Both parents and children should develop trust and faith so they can discuss any situation without any hindrance. Parents should not take failures very seriously and encourage their children to explore new things and do well. Remember, if life exists, anything is possible. A child should have the courage to accept his faults or limitations, and parents must encourage such acts. If they have trust, parents and children can create an encouraging atmosphere so that the assessment of capabilities can be done better. If a rabbit starts feeling disappointed because he is not as strong as an elephant, then the rabbit will always remain dejected. A rabbit needs to understand its strengths and be happy that it can run much faster than an elephant. A rabbit should always participate in running competitions rather than in wrestling championships.

A Word for Teachers

Teaching or imparting knowledge is the noblest profession in the world. I understand it well, as I have been an instructor, and my father was also a teacher. I can appreciate the amount of responsibility this profession carries. Teaching is about more than academics or imparting knowledge through books. A teacher must remember that they are shaping a life with their knowledge. They need to shape it well, as this life is the future. A teacher must remember that he makes himself immortal with his knowledge and teachings. Great teachers have always been remembered for their teachings and when their students do well.

Teachers must understand that teaching is more than just a job for earning money. It goes beyond that – it's about shaping futures and making a positive impact. Students rely on teachers for guidance, support, education, and assistance when needed. Students make mistakes and may lose their way at times. It's the teacher's role to help them get back on track. A teacher may use a gentle or firm approach to guide them, but it's crucial to remember that students are not hardcore criminals and should be treated with care and consideration. A teacher should employ various strategies to support students, whether using rewards or discipline. Even though students in higher grades may seem mature due to hormonal and physical changes in the body, they remain as vulnerable as they were in earlier years. Therefore, teachers need to handle student issues with care and understanding. Teachers need to act as parents to students.

Students who are in the process of graduating are in a transitional phase; they are no longer children but are not fully mature yet. Hormonal changes during this time can significantly affect a student's psychology. Many students need clarification about their careers and futures at this stage. While each student wants to succeed, they have different capabilities and focuses. This is where the role of a teacher becomes crucial. Teachers must guide students, show them the right path, and clear any confusion. Students, especially those living in hostels away from their families, struggle to handle the pressures of studies and general life. Just a few months ago, these students were carefree and surrounded by family and childhood friends, but now they feel lonely and burdened by their studies. They require the support of their teachers during this critical time.

If someone joins the teaching profession to earn money and does not understand student psychology, they are in the wrong profession. Whether in primary, secondary, or vocational education; a teacher's role in shaping a student's life and career remains paramount.

Arjuna from the Mahabharata would not have become a great warrior if he had not been supported and guided by his Guru, Dronacharya (teacher). Most of the time, a teacher plays a much more critical role than parents in carving one's life.

Being Perfectionist

Nothing is perfect in anybody's life. We all have our share of imperfections. Life is not just black or white; it is full of shades of grey. Even the best business people and leaders do not achieve perfection. Perfection is just a word, not a target. Yes, imperfections can create anxiety, fear, loneliness, and mental health issues, but if we accept the fact that nothing is perfect, we can deal with imperfections more easily. We must look at those living poorer lives than us, yet some are very happy.

When someone ends their life prematurely, they do not solve any problems; instead, they create more problems for their family members. It leaves a lasting impact on the hearts of their loved ones. **Failures should not be taken too seriously. Rather, the lessons learnt from failures should be taken seriously to avoid repeating the same mistakes**. It's important to remember that **suicide does not solve anything; it only creates new problems** for those who are left behind.

During challenging times, it's crucial for individuals to seek assistance. When confusion sets in, it becomes difficult to understand the underlying issues. It's essential to reach out to someone you trust and feel a strong connection with to seek counsel and support.

Takeaways from Chapter-4

- It's important to remember that the feeling of dejection is temporary. It's crucial to remain calm and patient during difficult times, allowing the situation to improve.

- Impulsive decision-making about life events should be avoided, as it's essential to consider each situation carefully.

- Success and failure are integral parts of life. It's important to remember that nothing is more significant than living a fulfilling life; everything else comes second.

- Life is not a linear journey; it resembles a zigzag line. When facing uncertainty or a lack of clarity, it's best to focus on the immediate next steps rather than looking too far ahead.

- As social beings, we often take events in the public sphere to heart. Whether it's an insult or praise, it profoundly impacts us.

- It's crucial to approach failures and successes gracefully, accepting them as part of life and using them as opportunities to learn and grow.

- Regarding ethical decisions, it's valuable to remember that right or wrong can be subjective and depend on individual perspectives.

- Expectations are natural in life, originating from family, friends, and ourselves. However, taking them with a pinch of salt and being mindful of the impact of excessive expectations and comparisons are essential.

- Understanding our capabilities and avoiding over estimation is vital in making realistic assessments.

- Teachers play a crucial role in shaping the future by impacting the lives of their students. Teaching is not just a profession but a calling to make a positive difference.

- Nobody is perfect and life is full of complexity and uncertainty. Instead of dwelling on failures, it's important to learn from them and strive to improve.
- It's essential to remember that no matter how difficult things may seem, resorting to suicide only perpetuates pain and creates new challenges for those left behind.

CHAPTER 5

FITNESS: THE ULTIMATE TREASURE

Let's Talk Fitness

I should have written this chapter at the beginning because one's fitness should be the top priority in life. I am writing this chapter at the end so that it can have a long-lasting impact on your mind. Work, marriage, and social life are only helpful if you are fit and healthy. Most of us ignore this fact and keep running behind materialistic targets. Whatever money you earn, or your success has no value if you are not healthy and fit.

I am surprised when I see people accepting their ill health or even lifestyle diseases like diabetes, heart issues, backache, and knee pain as part of their life and blaming it on age factor or fate. They don't even believe in trying to get rid of such problems. The sole activity they seem to engage in is the continuous consumption of pills as a solution to their issues. In my opinion, accepting any preventable sickness is a crime. Instead, knowingly allowing any illness or disease to happen is a crime. We should care for our health and not let it go wrong. Still, if something happens to us knowingly or unknowingly, treatment for that kind of illness/disease should be the top priority in one's life until it is cured. Just popping up a few tablets and capsules won't make it right. Medication can only suppress it for some time but can never cure it permanently. You can cure it or avoid it by changing your lifestyle. I understand that managing health-related things and work life is challenging but remember it is not impossible. Living each day mindfully, it can be achieved.

In today's fast-paced world, where everyone is racing ahead without a clear direction, the importance of fitness becomes even more critical. Many people are focused on achieving extreme wealth and success quickly, often at the expense of their physical and mental well-being. They are willing to sacrifice their health for financial and material rewards. It's important to remember that nothing is enjoyable if you are not in good health. No amount of money can be enjoyed from a hospital bed. Unfortunately, many of us only realise the importance of fitness when it's too late. **One of India's most successful investors Rakesh Jhunjhunwala – said something that really stood out. He said, "My worst investment has been my health. I would encourage everybody to invest the most in that"**. With his statement on health, it was very clear that the man, who is worth more than Rs 21,000 crore, wasn't happy about his health.

Is it so difficult to be fit and successful at the same time? No, not at all. It's simply a matter of making fitness a habit and prioritising health. Once you've made fitness a habit, you can enjoy success and a social life. Why do I keep using the word 'habit'? Because if you incorporate fitness into your daily life, like brushing your teeth, washing your hands, or getting ready for work, you can stay fit with minimal effort. Many of us prioritise investing time and energy in what to wear to a party over our fitness. Sometimes, we spend more time researching a car that will last 15 to 20 years than we do thinking about our bodies, which we expect to use for 70 to 80 years. We may blame our tight work schedules, the environment, poor quality food, karma, or even God for poor health. Still, we often fail to acknowledge our poor eating habits or rough, unorganised, and indisciplined lifestyles.

Many of us have extensive knowledge about cricket, football, space and rocket science, the politics of our own country, and world politics. However, we often lack sufficient knowledge about our own bodies. We tend to misuse, ill-treat, and abuse our bodies, taking them for granted. While our bodies can tolerate mistreatment and abuse for a long time, they will eventually show symptoms before breaking down. Everyone must understand how our bodies function and know about fundamental health-related issues. Fortunately, numerous resources are available today to learn about our bodies, health, and fitness. It is our responsibility to educate ourselves and take care of our bodies.

Understanding Fitness

Before we go any further, I'd like to make a disclaimer. I am not a doctor or a fitness expert, but I have always been passionate about fitness. The information I will share is based on my personal experiences and knowledge gained on my fitness journey. I have always prioritised fitness and am excited to share what I've learnt.

There are three ways to assess your fitness: 1. Organ function, 2. Frequency of illness, fatigue, or lethargy, and 3. Recovery speed from sickness.

First, it can be challenging to assess the well-being of our internal organs without clinical tests, but the health and functionality of our external organs can provide some insight. Regular medical checkups, including blood and urine tests, are essential for understanding internal organ health. People's energy levels and daily functioning can also explain their internal health. Additionally, physical appearance and skin texture can indicate overall health. Symptoms such as fatigue, breathlessness, lethargy, and anxiety may suggest underlying health issues. Acknowledging that poor mental health can ultimately affect physical well-being over time is essential.

Secondly, how often do you get sick? If you get sick very frequently, it may indicate that your body cannot handle even minor temperature, location, or weather changes. People who experience frequent illnesses such as coughs, colds, body aches, stomach upsets, or seasonal fevers may be more prone to these issues.

Third, recovery from illness is significant because it shows the immune system's strength. Even a tiny mistake can lead to disease, but a strong body can recover quickly. This shows inner strength. After having COVID-19, many seemingly healthy people experienced severe health issues during their recovery. A slow recovery indicates a weak immune system. People with weak immune systems often struggle to recover from illness and may be prone to catching diseases frequently.

A person's energy level and ability to perform daily functions indicate their fitness. Therefore, the frequency of illness and the speed of recovery can provide insight into a person's fitness level.

Importance of What We Eat

There are two critical components to fitness: diet and physical activity. While both are important, diet plays a more significant role, accounting for about 80% of our fitness goals. This doesn't mean that physical training is less important; it's still crucial for achieving fitness goals. However, **our fitness journey begins with what we eat and how we eat (at what time).** This 80:20 ratio emphasises the significant impact of our diet on our fitness journey compared to physical activity. Many people think that one hour of exercise gives them a free pass to eat whatever they want and the way they want. However, it's not a balanced approach to fitness if, for example, you eat high-calorie foods and then try to burn off those calories through exercise. Many neglect proper nutrition and meal timing, which are equally crucial for fitness. Our fitness journey is based on a combination of three key components: a well-balanced diet that provides the necessary nutrients, diet time, and regular physical activity to maintain overall health and well-being. Therefore, our overall health depends on: -

- Eating Habits/ Discipline
- Physical Health
- Mental Health

The most neglected aspect out of the three is our eating habits. Eating is not just about filling our stomachs. Consuming the right nutritional foods at the correct times can improve physical and mental health. I have experimented with various eating habits based on my work schedule, including six mini meals, three big meals, a low-carb/keto diet, and more. These trials taught me that some approaches were ineffective or unsustainable, while others served as short-term solutions. There's no one-size-fits-all solution, as different body types respond differently to the same diet. Sometimes, we need personalised solutions based on our body type and work schedules. That's why I aim to educate you on the fundamentals of fitness rather than provide a one-size-fits-all formula for staying fit.

Insulin Resistance

Glucose is a type of sugar that our bodies get from the food and drinks we consume, and it serves as the body's primary energy source. Blood sugar, also known as blood glucose, refers to the amount of glucose present in our blood. This glucose is responsible for providing energy to our bodies, and maintaining the proper blood sugar levels is crucial for our overall health. Insulin is a hormone produced by the pancreas's beta cells. When blood glucose levels rise, such as after eating, insulin is released from Pancreas into the blood to lower the glucose levels. Insulin helps the glucose enter the body's cells, which can be used for energy or stored for later use. **Understanding the role of blood sugar and insulin is essential for our overall health and well-being.**

[xv]When we consume foods such as rice, bread, or other high-carbohydrate options, digestion begins in the stomach and small intestine. During this process, the carbohydrates are broken down and absorbed into the bloodstream as glucose. Due to glucose in bloodstream, our blood sugar levels rise. In reaction to that, the pancreas releases insulin, a hormone, to help regulate and facilitate the absorption of glucose into the body's cells, including the liver, muscle, and fat tissues. This process ensures that our blood sugar levels return to their normal state after we eat.

In a healthy individual, insulin plays a crucial role in enabling cells to take up glucose from the bloodstream. However, when there is an excess of glucose, the over-secretion of insulin can occur. This can lead to an increase in the production of fat in the body and a decrease in the breakdown of fat, contributing to fat accumulation in body tissues.

If the sugar in the blood is not effectively processed, possibly due to insufficient insulin secretion or resistance to insulin's action, blood sugar levels may not decrease as expected after eating. Consistently high blood sugar levels several hours after eating may indicate a susceptibility to diabetes. To mitigate this risk and maintain good health, choosing foods that do not cause sudden, extreme spikes in blood sugar levels is essential. Opting for balanced and nutritious food choices can help regulate blood sugar levels and support overall well-being.

Insulin's primary role is to normalise the blood sugar spikes that occur after eating. Different types of food can lead to varying levels of blood sugar spikes. For example, glucose causes the highest spike, represented by the value 1, while other foods cause less significant spikes, represented by a fraction of 1.

The Glycemic Index (GI) is a scale that measures how much a particular food increases blood sugar levels. For example, pure glucose has a Glycemic Index of 1 (it is used as reference point), while other foods have values less than 1, such as 0.8, 0.5, or 0.3. Choosing foods with a lower Glycemic Index can help regulate blood sugar levels and prevent sharp spikes. By consuming foods with a lower Glycemic Index, the body needs to produce less insulin, which reduces the strain on the pancreas. This means the pancreas doesn't have to work extra hard to generate insulin. Opting for foods with a lower Glycemic Index, which causes lower sugar level spikes, can help the body avoid the need to produce extra insulin to counteract high blood sugar levels. It's essential to be mindful of excessive blood sugar spikes and insulin levels, as they can have detrimental effects on overall health.

The GI ranges[xvi] are defined as follows: -

- **Low GI: 55 or below** – These foods have the least impact on blood sugar.
- **Medium GI: 56 to 69** – Foods in this range cause a moderate increase in blood sugar.
- **High GI: 70 to 100** – These items lead to the most significant blood sugar spikes.

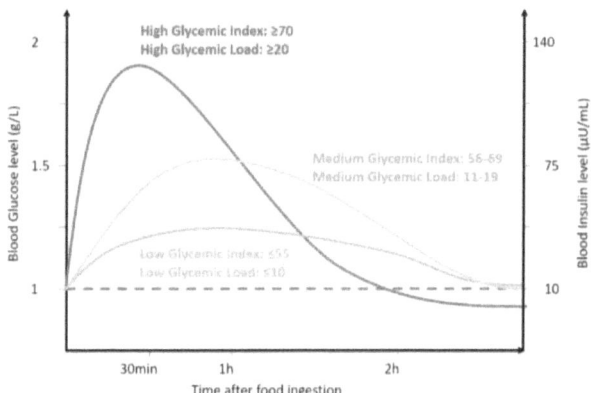

Consuming high Glycemic index foods due to our lifestyle or food habits puts an extra load on the pancreas gland, leading to increased insulin release. This additional supply of insulin creates blood sugar resistance to insulin and a higher demand for insulin. This irregular insulin release slowly leads to insulin resistance in the body.

A high level of insulin blocks the fat-burning process in the body and results in the deposition of extra fats in the body. Extra fat in the body and insulin resistance can result in diabetes, thyroid issues, and blood pressure problems. **Insulin resistance occurs when cells in our muscles, fat, and liver do not respond well to insulin and cannot easily take glucose from our blood.** As a result, our pancreas produces more insulin to help glucose enter our cells. If our pancreas can produce enough insulin to compensate for our cells' weak response, our blood glucose levels will stay healthy; otherwise, pre-diabetic conditions may develop. In this state, blood glucose levels remain higher than usual and may eventually progress into a full-fledged diabetic condition.

Now, you might ask me the most challenging question. "Which food items have a low Glycemic index?" The answer is straightforward….. "Search on Google" (ha ha ha). This was on a lighter note, but it is effortless, and you can find it on Google. As a general rule, all the natural things produced by nature, like vegetables and most fruits, are low in the Glycemic index. All artificial processed food, packed or tinned drinks and liquor are very high on the Glycemic index.

Some foods are high in the Glycemic index. Still, when consumed with certain other foods, they become moderate on the glycemic index, e.g. White rice is high on the Glycemic index. Still, when consumed with Pulses and veggies as a meal, it becomes a moderate Glycemic index food because of the supplementary action of proteins. **Pulses** are rich in proteins but are deficient in sulphur-containing amino acids like methionine and cysteine. **Cereals** are deficient in the amino acid lysine. When pulses and cereals are taken together, they have a synergistic effect as the limiting amino acid of one is supplemented by the other. This property is known as **supplementary action of proteins**[xvii].

While some people avoid white rice due to its high Glycemic index and perceived lack of healthiness, it's perfectly fine to consume it when paired with pulses and vegetables. Understanding how our bodies react to food is essential, so it's important to research and raise awareness for ourselves. Instead of waiting for others to provide healthy food, we should be mindful and informed about our food choices and their potential effects on our well-being. Homemade foods, which are naturally grown, are the best option, while processed and packaged foods containing added chemicals should be limited due to their potential harm.

When we consume fat, it undergoes a different digestive process compared to carbohydrates. Instead of breaking down into glucose, fat is metabolised differently and does not directly cause an increase in blood glucose levels. Consuming a meal or snack with moderate fat, protein, and fibre can contribute to more stable blood glucose levels. This is because fat, protein, and fibre collectively work to slow down the digestion process, which in turn delays the absorption of carbohydrates and helps prevent sudden spikes in blood glucose levels.

However, it's essential to be mindful of the type and quantity of fat consumed. Opting for heart-healthy fats and being cautious with saturated and trans-fats is critical. These unhealthy fats not only have high-calorie content but also tend to have a high Glycemic index, which can negatively impact blood glucose levels. Therefore, it's advisable to limit or avoid foods containing saturated and trans-fats to maintain overall heart health and manage blood glucose levels effectively.

Lately, I've noticed a concerning trend among people aged 16 to 35. They prefer consuming more processed and fast food over homemade, simple meals. This age group tends to favour outside food and often prefers the taste of such food over simpler homemade options. Their diet includes high consumption of items like potato chips, finger chips, burgers, pizzas, momos, samosas, and pakodas, as well as aerated drinks and alcohol. These foods are high in the Glycemic index, saturated fats, trans-fats, and calories, contributing to the increasing numbers of overweight and obese individuals in this age group. The high Basal Metabolic Rate (BMR) in this age bracket often delays the harmful effects of processed food and drinks. By the time the adverse effects become apparent, it's usually too late to reverse the damage. This issue is not only limited to the 16 to 35 age group, as even children are facing obesity problems due to excess consumption of fast foods. Child obesity is on rise significantly. Just check these certain facts[xviii] about obesity: -

- In 2022, 1 in 8 people in the world were living with obesity.
- Worldwide adult obesity has more than doubled since 1990, and adolescent obesity has quadrupled.
- In 2022, 2.5 billion adults (18 years and older) were overweight. Of these, 890 million were living with obesity.
- In 2022, 43% of adults aged 18 years and over were overweight and 16% were living with obesity.
- In 2022, 37 million children under the age of 5 were overweight.
- Over 390 million children and adolescents aged 5–19 years were overweight in 2022, including 160 million who were living with obesity.

The general trend of consuming chips or packed snacks, eating out, or ordering food instead of preparing it at home, along with high alcohol/aerated drinks consumption and late-night eating, is on the rise. It is challenging to determine the exact frequency with which the average Indian family eats out, as this can vary widely depending on factors such as income level, location, and personal preference. However, according to a survey conducted by the National Restaurant Association of India (NRAI)[xix] in 2019, 34% of Indian consumers eat out at least once a month, while 27% eat out once every two months, and 16% eat out once every three months. **This suggests that a significant portion of the population does eat out on a regular basis.** Now the eating out trend has increased to weekly or at times twice in a week. These numbers are on rise only and numbers of new eating joints are also on rise.

Feasting and Fasting

In the past, our ancestors typically began their day with their first meal around 8 or 9 am and had their last meal around 5 or 6 pm. They lived in villages or remote places, and the availability of sunlight influenced their meal times, as electricity was rare. They were early risers and used to go to bed early as they didn't have distractions like TV and social media. Due to their lifestyle, they naturally followed **a pattern of feasting and fasting, eating for 8 to 9 hours and giving their bodies a 15 to 16-hour rest**. The absence of electricity was a boon for them.

In modern times, intermittent fasting has become a widespread practice. It involves setting specific periods for eating (Feasting time) and not eating (Fasting time). I've understood the importance of fasting over feasting, as it allows our bodies to rest, digest food, and cleanse internal organs. During fasting, the body focuses on processing consumed food, absorbing nutrients from food, eliminating toxins and consuming excess fat. Eating at frequent intervals can lead to undigested food accumulating in the body, causing issues such as bloating, gas, and constipation. It's essential to give our bodies time to carry out the cleansing process, just as we clean our houses daily to prevent dust and bacteria buildup. Sticking to a consistent fasting or feasting schedule is essential, with a bit of flexibility of plus or minus one hour if needed. This rhythm helps our bodies align with our biological clock, making digestion more efficient and enabling our bodies to extract maximum nutrition from the food we consume.

Intermittent fasting and Ketosis

There are several methods for practicing intermittent fasting. Some people choose to follow a 16:8 or 14:10 fasting to feasting ratio. Let's look at the 16:8 fasting method as an example. With this approach, one restricts their eating window to 8 hours and fasts for the remaining 16 hours, consuming only water. This method is known for its ability to promote rapid fat loss and aid in the removal of toxins from the body. By allowing the body time to cleanse and recover, intermittent fasting can act as a healing process.

Our bodies consist primarily of bones, muscles, and fat cells. It's important to understand that fat and weight loss are not the same. While weight loss can occur with the loss of muscle mass, fat loss is more significant as it specifically targets the reduction of excess fat in the body. Losing muscle mass can lead to sagging skin and accelerate ageing, while fat loss solely focuses on eliminating excess fat.

During fasting, the body turns to stored fats as its energy source after using available dietary carbohydrates (carbs), stored carbs (glycogen), and dietary fats. This shift from carbs to fats for energy is known as Ketosis. **Ketosis occurs when the body primarily relies on stored fats for fuel**.

Typically, the body uses blood sugar (glucose) as its primary energy source, which comes from starches and sugars found in carbohydrates. Carbohydrates are broken down into glucose, used as fuel for everyday activities. The liver stores glucose as glycogen and releases it when the body needs energy. Once the body has used up dietary carbs, stored glucose, and dietary fats (usually within 12 hours after a meal), it begins to utilise fat cells for energy. Fat cells are broken down into a compound called ketones, and the body then uses these ketones as an energy source.

Our liver naturally produces a small number of ketones. However, when our glucose levels decrease and our insulin levels drop, our liver increases the production of ketones to provide enough energy for our brain. This leads to high levels of ketones in our blood during ketosis.

You may have heard of the Ketogenic (keto) diet. This is a diet where one takes control of their body's energy source by consuming a low-carb (50-130 grams of carbs per day) and high-protein and high-fat diet. This triggers ketosis, a state where the body burns fats for energy in the absence of carbs. By following the Ketogenic diet, we force our body into ketosis by either eliminating or significantly reducing carb consumption, giving us the power to choose our body's energy source.

A long-term keto diet (20-50 grams of carbs per day) has its side effects. Carbs are a good energy source and should not be artificially removed. Depriving our body of carbohydrates may lead to a state of 'brain fog', which means slow processing by the brain. While all other organs can function on alternate energy sources, such as fats, some of the brain requires carbohydrates to function optimally. Without carbohydrates, we may experience dullness or a state of brain fog and find it difficult to concentrate on tasks requiring brain participation for an extended period. Even though our liver can store glucose as glycogen and provide energy to the brain, we should not deprive our bodies of carbohydrates. A diet without carbs is not sustainable for extended periods. **That is why I prefer intermittent fasting, where we don't deprive our body of**

carbohydrates but create a state of ketosis through fasting. Another advantage of fasting is that it helps our body naturally eliminate accumulated toxins. The brain largely depends on glucose for fuel on a standard low-carb diet.

One might initially feel a drop in energy levels due to fasting and a decrease in working efficiency. It might be a bit uncomfortable initially, but within seven to ten days, our bodies get used to it, and we should become more comfortable. There will be no signs of dullness or lethargy in the body during the fasting process. I've noticed that our bodies rejuvenate after a few days of fasting due to the production of newer cells. The face may appear more radiant due to the release of toxins and the elimination of excess fat cells from the body. People with skin disease problems, hair fall, pimples, or acne may find relief when they fast.

Intermittent fasting is a method I have tried and tested. I lost seven kilograms in three months without losing muscle mass. My body fat percentage dropped by 3%, and I lost fat around my waist. The muscle definition on my body became more prominent. Yes, intermittent fasting requires discipline and dedication to remain in a fasting state. It's essential to stay hydrated during this process. The feasting window can be chosen based on your schedule or work timings, but I suggest keeping the feasting window close to the period between sunrise and sunset. This period is when our bodies are primarily active, and due to the presence of sunlight, our metabolic rate also remains high.

No matter which fasting period you choose, it should be at least 12 hours with no food consumption (no calories) during this time. The main idea during fasting is to avoid consuming anything that raises blood sugar levels. Any calorie intake will increase blood sugar levels and disrupt the fasting process. Intermittent fasting is a method to regulate insulin release, which can help alleviate conditions such as hair loss, pimples, acne, diabetes, thyroid issues, and even high blood pressure. It is recognised that fasting for 16 hours may not be feasible for everyone daily, especially young professionals. Therefore, depending on work schedule, 12 to 14 hours of fasting one should aim at. A minimum 12-hour fasting period is recommended for a healthy lifestyle, and this is achievable. During a 12-hour fasting window, 7 to 8 hours are typically spent sleeping. The remaining 4 to 5 hours need to be managed before and after the sleep schedule. One needs to delay breakfast slightly later in the day and have dinner a few hours earlier. A bit of discipline and fasting can be well managed.

Some people follow the 5:2 or 6:1 fasting to-feasting regimen, which involves fasting for 24 hours once or twice a week. This can benefit those with busy schedules or frequent travel for work. They may consume only vegetable juices, less sugary fruits, or salads on fasting days.

Fasting has been found to help rejuvenate old cells and generate new ones in the body. This is due to the body's response to the fasting state, which can lead to cellular repair processes and changes in gene expression. In addition, **fasting has been shown to stimulate autophagy, a natural process through which the body removes damaged cells and replaces them with new ones, contributing to overall cellular rejuvenation**. Fasting holds the potential to be a powerful health tool by improving physical health and eliminating harmful cells from the body. It is believed that fasting can prevent the development of cancer cells or reduce the risk of chronic diseases like cancer, making it a compelling option for health-conscious individuals.

Ketogenesis xx

The brain is the only organ in the human body that needs carbohydrates (Glucose) to function. Reducing carb intake may initially lead to brain fog; the body typically adapts to this change within ten days. Low-carb diets work by providing energy to the brain through a process called ketogenesis. This process involves the liver producing ketones from fatty acids when glucose and insulin levels are low, allowing the brain to use ketones as an alternative fuel source. When an individual is fasting or has a low carb intake, the liver increases its production of ketones, supplying up to 75% of the brain's energy needs.

It's crucial to understand that while carbohydrates are not essential in large quantities, they still play a vital role in overall nutrition. In Indian diets, there's often a higher emphasis on carbohydrates and a lower intake of protein. This underscores the importance of customising diets to strike the right balance between carbohydrates and other essential nutrients, such as proteins. By doing so, we can ensure our diets are not only nourishing but also tailored to our individual needs.

Gluconeogenesis

Gluconeogenesis[xxi] (literally, "formation of new sugar") is the metabolic process by which glucose is formed from non-carbohydrate sources, such as lactate, amino acids, and glycerol.

Although most of the brain can use ketones, some portions of the brain require glucose to function. On a deficient-carb diet, some glucose can be supplied by the small amount of carbs consumed. The rest comes from a process in your body called **gluconeogenesis, which means "making new glucose."** In this process, the liver creates glucose for the brain to use. The liver makes the glucose using amino acids, the building blocks of protein. The liver can also make glucose from glycerol. Glycerol is the backbone that links fatty acids in triglycerides, the body's storage form of fat. **Thanks to gluconeogenesis, the portions of the brain that need glucose get a steady supply, even when our carb intake is deficient. Therefore, there is no need to**

worry about the brain when you are on a low-carb diet or intermittent fasting. It is just a tiring or lightheaded notion that one gets in the initial days. This tiring or lightheaded feeling is known as keto flu or low-carb flu. It is just a matter of time before our body gets used to fasting and does not demand carbs. In a few days only, low-carb flu symptoms will disappear.

Need for Carbohydrates and Sugars?

Carbohydrates and sugars play a crucial role as the body's favourite energy sources. Along with dietary intake, the body taps into stored carbohydrates (glycogen), dietary fats, proteins, and deposited body fats to meet its energy requirements. However, it prefers to utilise dietary carbohydrates and sugars first. This preference is due to the ease with which carbohydrates and sugars can be broken down into glucose, providing a quick energy source for the body. As a result, our bodies derive energy primarily from dietary carbohydrates and sugars.

Compared to fibres, proteins, or fats, the rapid absorption of carbs and sugars leads to a sharp increase in blood sugar levels. This spike triggers the pancreas to release additional insulin to regulate the blood sugar spike. However, with excessive intake, the body may become resistant to insulin, which can have severe effects on overall health, potentially leading to type2 diabetes. This underscores the importance of being mindful of our carbs and sugars intake for our overall health.

Various physiological processes influence the human body, and one aspect that has garnered attention is the addictive nature of carbohydrates and sugars. **Research suggests that the addictive potential of carbs and sugars may surpass that of narcotic drugs**. When consumed, carbohydrates and sugars trigger the release of dopamine, a neurotransmitter associated with pleasure and happiness. This release of dopamine can lead to cravings for more sugars and carbs, fostering an addictive cycle.

Furthermore, the rapid energy boost provided by carbs and sugars can contribute to excessive consumption. This overconsumption, compounded by their addictive qualities, can have detrimental effects on the body.

It is often argued that carbohydrates and sugars are crucial energy sources for the body and, therefore, should be a vital part of our diet. However, the body can meet its glucose needs without relying on carbs and sugars through processes like Ketogenesis and Gluconeogenesis. Consequently, it is important not to emphasise the significance of carbs and sugars overly. Overindulgence in carbs and sugars (found in items such as burgers, pizzas, bakery products, sweets, aerated drinks, and alcohol) can lead to various dietary and gastrointestinal disorders. Excessive consumption of carbs and sugars can also contribute to premature ageing and hinders muscle production.

Fruits and Dried Fruits

Fruits and dried fruits are incredibly beneficial for our health due to their rich nutrient content. They are excellent sources of essential micronutrients such as vitamins, minerals, proteins, healthy fats (un-saturated fats), and antioxidants. Fresh fruits are particularly advantageous because of their high water content and dietary fibre, which offer various health benefits. Despite these benefits, being mindful of their natural sugar content is essential.

Fruits and dried fruits contain sugars, including fructose, and excessive consumption can lead to overstimulation of the pancreas and result in excessive insulin release. Moderation is the key, especially when consuming sweet fruits like mangoes, grapes, and watermelon. Fresh fruits also serve as an excellent source of hydration due to their high water content, making them a great option to stay hydrated, particularly during the summer. Consuming fresh fruits and dried fruits in moderation is essential to prevent potential health issues such as fatty liver, diabetes, increased triglycerides, and excess belly fat due to excessive sugar and energy intake.

Glucose and Fructose Metabolism

Glucose is a simple sugar commonly found in carbohydrates and regular sugars. It is a primary energy source for the body and can be metabolised in every cell. On the other hand, fructose is another type of simple sugar, and it is present in honey, fruits, vegetables, and corn syrup. The metabolic process of fructose is different from that of glucose. Unlike glucose, fructose is primarily metabolised in specific tissues such as the liver, kidney, small intestine, adipose tissues, and muscles. Notably, the transport and metabolism of fructose do not require insulin, unlike glucose. It's worth noting that sweet fruits are abundant in both natural sugars and calories, making them a good source of sugar to satisfy sweet cravings while also providing essential nutrients and fibre.

Research has shown that excessive fructose consumption, especially in the form of sweet drinks like honey, corn syrup, and fruit juices, can have a detrimental effect on the body.

Scientific studies have consistently shown that high fructose consumption can have serious implications for liver health. When the liver is overwhelmed with high levels of fructose, it converts the excess sugar into fat through lipogenesis. This process, if not addressed, can lead to the development of non-alcoholic fatty liver disease over time. This condition is characterised by the unhealthy buildup of fat in liver cells, a situation that should be a cause of concern for those who regularly consume excessive fructose.

On a positive note, recent findings have shed light on the pivotal role of the gut in metabolising fructose post-consumption. In a remarkable display of self-preservation, the gut prioritises using fructose, thereby shielding the liver from potential fructose-induced harm. This discovery underscores the complex interplay between fructose consumption, gut function, and liver health, offering a glimmer of hope in our understanding of this process.

Fructose is a naturally occurring sugar found in fruits, fruit juices, certain vegetables, and honey. It can be a beneficial component of a well-rounded and healthy diet. However, increased fructose consumption has led to concerns about its impact on human health, particularly due to its widespread addition to processed foods. While natural sources of fructose can be part of a nutritious diet, it's essential to be mindful of high fructose corn syrup, which is derived from corn starch and added to less healthy foods such as sodas and candies. Despite the presence of fructose in these less nutritious foods, they can still be enjoyed in moderation.

'Maintenance' Calories

Let us understand 'maintenance' calories [xxii] and their significance so that we can use this figure to ascertain whether we need more or less calories for body weight maintenance, reduction or increase. Maintenance calories are also known as 'Total Daily Energy expenditure' (TDEE). If a person consumes calories equivalent to TDEE daily, his body weight will remain static. An increase and decrease in body weight will depend on whether that person consumes more or less than TDEE calories. The total amount of a person's TDEE comprises of the following: -

- Basal Metabolic rate (BMR)
- Non-Exercise Activity Thermogenesis (NEAT)
- The Thermic Effect of Feeding (TEF)

- And their Exercise Activity (EA), or Physical Activity Level (PAL)

Understanding an individual's calorie maintenance level is crucial for effective nutrition planning. It's important to note that this maintenance level isn't a fixed number but a range of approximately 200-300 calories. Total Daily Energy Expenditure (TDEE) can be calculated through various methods and easily found using a quick Google search. To calculate your TDEE, you must first determine your **Basal Metabolic Rate (BMR),** which can be done using any of the numerous online calculators available.

BMR[xxiii] is defined as the number of calories the body burns when it is at rest and performing essential life-sustaining functions. These functions include circulating blood, breathing, maintaining body temperature, nutrient processing and supporting basic cellular processes. BMR is often called the resting metabolic rate (RMR) because it measures the calories burned while the body is at rest, such as when a person is lying in bed all day. The BMR is essential because it represents the minimum energy required to keep the body functioning, regardless of physical activity levels.

I don't want to complicate things at this stage. Therefore, explanation of BMR and BMR variables are attached as **annexure** at the end of this book. I would recommend going through BMR calculation to understand calorie requirement of the body. This will help in understanding macro-nutrient requirement of the body.

Reduction in Calorie Intake

Intermittent fasting can be a helpful strategy for reducing calorie intake. Limiting the feasting period to 8 to 10 hours each day gives individuals a restricted window for consuming calories. When approaching meal choices consciously, such as opting for low-carb, high-quantity salads and vegetables and incorporating moderate to substantial amounts of protein and healthy fats; managing calorie intake within this limited timeframe effectively becomes feasible. This approach emphasises the importance of mindful eating and ensuring proper nutrition during feasting.

While there are various strategies for reducing calorie intake, one of the most effective ones is to prioritise vegetables and salads. For those who struggle with morning hunger, a practical approach is to consume only salads until noon, followed by an early lunch and early dinner. This strategy allows you to include a balanced mix of salads, proteins, fats, and carbs in diminishing proportions during both lunch and dinner. The salads, when consumed before carbohydrates, can help mitigate blood sugar spikes. The fibre content in salads creates a protective layer in the stomach, thereby slowing down carb absorption and limiting insulin release.

Shifting towards more plant-based diets over animal-based diets is also a valuable approach. Plant-based diets are generally easier to digest and have a lower Glycemic index, while animal-based diets takes considerable time to digest and often contain more calories due to the use of excessive spices and oil in the preparation of food. However, the most crucial aspect of all these strategies is to manage overall calorie intake. Successful weight management and achieving desired outcomes hinge on effectively managing your calorie intake in relation to your Basal Metabolic Rate (BMR) and activity level. By closely aligning calorie consumption with BMR and adjusting it according to one's activity level, one can make the process of weight management significantly more manageable and attainable.

Mindful Eating

Who wouldn't be a fan of the flavorful delights of Maggi noodles, crunchy samosas, cheesy pizzas, juicy burgers, and crispy pakodas? The indulgence doesn't stop there; the world of delicious eats is vast and diverse, guaranteed to make your mouth water.

Parties are often synonymous with clinking glasses filled with beer, smooth smoky whiskey, and fine wine. These lively gatherings usually kick off in the late evening and carry on well into the night or early morning hours. With parties, come a bountiful spread of rich, delectable foods and a steady flow of alcoholic beverages. As a result, calorie consumption can surge to ten times the norm compared to regular days. It's common for an individual to ingest up to 2000 calories in a single night of revelry, which may equal an entire day's calorie intake. In the spirit of celebration, healthy eating habits are often set aside, and mindful consumption of food and beverages takes a backseat.

For some, attending such festivities is a matter of personal choice, driven by an insatiable appetite for a good time. However, in many cases, social obligations dictate participation in these gatherings. Regardless of the reason for attending, the outcome remains the same – the consumption of excess calories. In fact, the calorie intake during a single party often surpasses what one might consume over the course of three regular days. Over time, this surplus of calories contributes to the accumulation of unwanted belly fat and the infamous double chin. By being mindful of our consumption, we can take control of our health and prevent these issues.

To mitigate the potential adverse effects of partying, it's essential to be mindful of our dietary choices before, during and after attending social events. While altogether avoiding parties may not always be feasible, it's crucial to consider the impact of our actions. Before attending any gathering, it's advisable to maintain a lean diet with minimal calories to create a buffer for any indulgences at the event. This could involve regulating calorie intake by consuming a balanced diet and exercising portion control.

For example, if you have an evening event, it's essential to maintain a sense of balance throughout the day. If you find it challenging to limit food consumption before the party, it's reassuring to know that you can still exercise restraint during the event. After the party, the focus should shift to restoring balance and well-being. This can be achieved by consuming hydrating beverages and light nutritious foods, allowing you to enjoy the event without the guilt of overindulgence.

The key is aligning our calorie intake with our body's needs. This requires a sense of self-awareness and conscious eating habits, which can significantly contribute to our overall well-being and fitness. It's a reminder that we hold the power to make healthy choices, even during social gatherings. Neglecting this responsibility could lead to severe health consequences, but staying aware and responsible can maintain our health and enjoy social events guilt-free.

Despite attempts to restrict calorie intake both before and after a social gathering, the harmful consequences of overindulging in food and alcohol can linger for several days. Coping with these effects may demand even more substantial efforts to bounce back from the party's aftermath. Acknowledging that socialising can be fulfilling through other avenues aside from excessive eating and drinking is essential. An exceptional hiking pleasure trip can be as delightful as a festive party. While it may not be feasible to substitute a birthday celebration with a hiking trip, we can certainly consider the timing of our festivities. Instead of hosting late evening or nighttime parties, we can organise extravagant lunches and enjoyable daytime gatherings. By being mindful of these details, we can create memorable experiences for everyone involved.

Stay Physically Active

Maintaining overall health involves more than just eating right. In addition to a nutritious diet, adequate physical activity and good quality sleep are crucial for fitness. Physical activity plays a key role in preventing chronic diseases such as heart disease, diabetes, and obesity. It also contributes to improved cardiovascular health, a more robust immune system, and a reduced risk of various health conditions. **On the other hand, good quality sleep significantly impacts mental well-being.**

When one commits to maintaining a balanced and nutritious diet, they take a significant step towards embarking on a journey to better fitness. Adequate sleep, regular physical activity, and healthy eating habits are crucial in providing the body with the necessary strength and immunity to combat diseases and illnesses. In addition to bolstering one's defences against infection, engaging in physical activity facilitates a speedier recovery from health setbacks. Furthermore, physical activity not only aids in burning calories but also elevates the body's metabolic rate. Even during rest periods, the body continues to burn calories at an accelerated pace due to the metabolic boost derived from physical activity.

Engaging in regular physical activity has been found to have a significant impact on mental well-being. Research indicates that individuals who incorporate physical activity into their lifestyles tend to report higher happiness and mental resilience levels. Furthermore, physical activity contributes to better external health and plays a crucial role in enhancing internal organ function. It promotes enhanced bone density, increased joint mobility, and improved muscle strength. Strength training can have an anti-aging effect on the body by preserving and restoring muscle mass and contributing to the body's ability to regenerate new cells.

Engaging in regular physical activity has been found to enhance cognitive functions significantly. This includes improvements in memory, attention, and problem-solving skills. Physical activity is also known to stimulate the growth of new nerve cells and enhance brain agility.

When it comes to fitness and physical activity, it's essential to prioritise our health over luxury. Instead of investing in expensive shoes or fitness outfits, investing in our well-being is more crucial. Many people approach their fitness journey as if they are preparing for a special event, splurging on costly gym memberships and fancy workout gear. However, starting by developing a fitness habit and focusing on the basics is essential. Progress may be slow, but consistency is critical to maintain a healthy routine.

Disciplined Eating and Physical Workout

As I have previously mentioned, it is essential to acknowledge that favourable outcomes are not immediate but result from dedication, consistency, and disciplined effort. The pursuit of fitness demands a rigorous commitment to the cultivation of beneficial habits. It is noteworthy that physical well-being can significantly enhance personal presentation; therefore, the correlation between fitness and sartorial elegance is undeniable. Moreover, an individual's fitness and overall health reflect their character, unwavering resolve, discipline, and mindfulness. Notably, the pursuit of fitness enhances conscious awareness and profoundly augments cognitive capacities. Indeed, fitness is a virtue that exponentially fortifies an individual's character. Consequently, prioritising fitness inevitably leads to acquiring the skills necessary to uphold physical well-being.

In his 'Chanakya Neeti', Chanakya advises, (I quote) **"Hunger is common for any living being. But only a few get to enjoy plenty of delicious food. Even if you get food, there is no guarantee that you will enjoy it. If one is ill and does not have an appetite, what is the use of getting delicious food?"** (unquote). In short, he had also emphasised being fit to enjoy delicious food.

Yoga/ Cardio/ Weight Training

Everyone has their own preferences regarding staying fit, and it's important to respect that. There are so many different ways to stay in shape because we all have different bodies and health needs. Staying disciplined is critical to achieving fitness goals, which means following a balanced and consistent routine. Whether it's running, walking, weight training, practicing Yoga, or martial arts, people can choose the activities that best suit their preferences. Some enjoy outdoor activities such as walking, hiking, and running, while others prefer intense weight training. Some find satisfaction in an hour of sweating on the treadmill, while others love stretching out on their yoga mat and practicing yoga poses and breathing exercises. It's all about finding what brings joy and wellness to your life. Remember that no single exercise can provide all the benefits; both aerobic and anaerobic exercises have advantages and disadvantages.

I have always been passionate about fitness and strength training, finding joy in lifting weights and embracing the challenge of working with dumbbells and barbells. However, there was a time when I didn't appreciate the practice of Yoga and couldn't quite comprehend its scientific principles. Surprisingly, my perspective has completely changed in recent years, and I have developed a deep love for Yoga. Nowadays, I incorporate Yoga into my fitness routine alongside my weight training regimen, finding balance and fulfillment in both practices.

To maintain overall physical wellbeing, it is beneficial to incorporate both weightlifting, which focuses on strength training, and Yoga, which emphasises flexibility and strength training, into your fitness routine. Weightlifting is essential for enhancing bone density, strength, and muscle mass. On the other hand, Yoga plays a pivotal role in improving flexibility and joint mobility by strengthening the elasticity of muscles and joints within the body. Additionally, various yoga poses help strengthen muscles and promote mental relaxation. The combination of denser bones and well-developed muscles contributes to the body's structural strength, protecting against diseases and illnesses. Furthermore, it supports the recovery of damaged tissues. The body's mobility relies heavily on the elasticity of muscles, which can be improved through regular yoga-asanas.

When incorporating Pranayama with yoga-asanas, individuals can experience a reduction in their breathing rate while achieving regulation of the respiratory system. This leads to a balanced and tranquil breathing pattern, which benefits the optimal functioning of different bodily organs and imparts an anti-ageing influence. Consequently, the fusion of weight training and Yoga Pranayama techniques is poised to yield exceptional and transformative outcomes.

While I don't oppose running or high-intensity interval training (HIIT) as part of a well-rounded fitness routine, it's essential to consider the potential drawbacks of these activities. Running and HIIT are effective forms of cardiovascular exercise that can aid in fat-burning and weight loss. However, certain risks are associated with these high-impact activities, mainly when they are not performed in a controlled manner.

Individuals who engage in HIIT or long-distance running should prioritise regular medical check-ups to monitor their overall health and well-being. If not approached with caution and consideration for individual health conditions, these types of vigorous exercises can potentially lead to elevated blood pressure and even increase the risk of heart attacks.

While HIIT has gained popularity for its ability to deliver quick fitness results within a condensed timeframe, it's also worth noting that it's essential to strike a balance between achieving short-term goals and maintaining long-term health. As with any exercise regimen, it's crucial to approach HIIT and running with mindfulness and awareness of potential risks.

In addition to aiding in fat burning, it's important to note that cardio exercises also burn muscle mass and reduce bone density. As a result, it's advisable to incorporate cardio exercises after weight training sessions, particularly for shorter durations. This sequencing effectively amplifies the fat-burning process without compromising muscle mass. Solely relying on cardio workouts may lead to reductions in muscle mass and bone density and may have implications for joint health, particularly in the knees and ankles. To mitigate these effects, it's beneficial to integrate cardio exercises with either weight training or Yoga, or even better, a combination of weight training, cardio, and Yoga.

In addition to regular exercise, it is highly recommended to incorporate long-distance walking, hiking, and jogging into your overall physical activity routine. Combining weight training with Yoga has been proven to significantly improve physical and mental well-being, leading to enhanced stability and overall health. Participation in Yoga has been linked to increase in blood circulation and improved skin health. As a result, individuals who regularly practice Yoga often enjoy the benefits of glowing and smooth skin more than those who do not engage in this practice.

Mental Health

Mental health and physical health are intricately connected and crucial for an individual's overall well-being. Adequate nutrition is essential for promoting good physical and psychological health. It is important to focus on consuming a balanced diet of natural and nutritious foods. Additionally, engaging in regular physical activity has been shown to have numerous benefits for mental health. Furthermore, quality sleep that is uninterrupted and restful is fundamental for maintaining optimal mental and physical health.

Improving mental health can be supported by developing strong communication skills. Effective communication can reduce the likelihood of conflicts and misunderstandings with others, which in turn can positively impact mental well-being. When people experience stress or struggle to find peace of mind, they may turn to alcohol or smoking as coping mechanisms. However, it's essential to avoid these substances when feeling stressed, as they can increase mental pressure and hurt mental health. The mind and body are intricately connected, and mental health issues can have physical manifestations, such as headaches, digestive problems, and sleep disturbances. Chronic stress and mental health disorders can weaken the immune system, making individuals more vulnerable to illnesses and hindering the body's ability to heal. Poor mental health can also lead to neglect of physical health and an increased tendency to engage in alcohol and smoking.

Understanding the interplay between mental and physical wellness is critical to overall well-being. It is essential to consider all aspects of life to enhance mental health, including professional, social, marital, financial, and physical well-being. A holistic approach prioritises health's physical and psychological aspects. Research shows that individuals who are satisfied with their work, have fulfilling relationships, maintain a solid financial foundation, and prioritise physical fitness are more likely to experience positive mental health. Therefore, investing in fitness and prioritising it as a primary goal in life is crucial. Interestingly, investing in fitness can yield greater returns than traditional financial investments, making it a valuable and worthwhile endeavour. **Investment in fitness always gives positive results**.

Simple Steps for Staying Healthy

While I generally don't endorse taking shortcuts, I want to share some straightforward tips that can help you improve your overall health and fitness. These tips are:-

- To start your day on a healthy note, consider having a big glass of lukewarm or room-temperature water. For added benefits, you can squeeze some fresh lemon juice into the water and add a pinch of turmeric powder. This simple morning ritual can help cleanse your digestive system and keep your body hydrated. Additionally, it may contribute to smoother bowel movements, promoting overall digestive wellness.

- In the morning, please refrain from consuming any tea or coffee that contains milk and sugar. If you feel the need, you may opt for a cup of unsweetened black tea, green tea, or coffee (without milk) later in the morning. It is recommended to avoid consuming any tea or coffee until 3 to 4 hours after waking up.

- During fasting, staying well-hydrated is important. Increase your water intake and drink regularly. This will help cleanse your digestive system and intestine and support your overall well-being.

- Break your fast and start your feasting period with a refreshing green salad to stimulate your appetite and provide essential nutrients.

- It is recommended to have a glass of water either 45 minutes before or 45 minutes after your meal. Avoid drinking water during or immediately after a meal, as it may lead to bloating.

- It's important to note that consuming salads 15 to 30 minutes before your main meal is beneficial as it allows for better digestion. Ensuring that you chew your salads properly aids to digestion and creates a protective layer in your tummy so that carbs and sugar absorption become slow. It's also worth remembering that the digestion process for cooked and raw food differs, and therefore, they should not be combined and should be eaten separately.

- When it comes to consuming food, it's best to follow a balanced approach that includes a variety of elements. Start with a generous portion of fresh salads and vegetables to provide essential nutrients and fibre. Then, incorporate a moderate serving of high-quality proteins such as lean meats, fish, eggs, or legumes to support muscle health. Next, include a reasonable amount of healthy fats from sources like avocados, nuts, seeds, and Desi Ghee/ butter for optimal nutrient absorption and satiety. Follow this with a controlled portion of complex carbohydrates from whole grains, or starchy vegetables to provide sustained energy. Finally, you can enjoy a small serving of a satisfying dessert or sweet treat to indulge your taste buds in moderation. Remember to be mindful of your overall portion sizes to support a healthy and balanced approach to eating.

- Include a variety of nuts and fruits in your daily diet and enjoy them as a snack between 4 and 5 p.m. Soaked nuts are recommended as they are easier to digest and provide more nutrients. After breaking your fast, you can also have nuts in the morning to kick start your day with a healthy and satisfying snack.

- Try to complete your evening meal around sunset or, at the latest by 8 pm. It's best to have a light dinner containing fewer carbohydrates and more of veggies/ soups.

- Remember to minimise your water intake before bedtime to avoid disrupting your sleep with frequent bathroom trips. Instead, it's better to stay hydrated by drinking water regularly during the day.

- You should ensure that you do not consume any calorie between the last bite of dinner and the first bite of your first meal the next day. This practice of fasting should be observed with the same discipline and respect as we do during religious fasts.

- As you begin fasting, you should commence with 12 hours of complete fasting, during which you consume only water. After this initial period, consider gradually extending the fasting window to 14 to 16 hours. Fasting for 14 hours can be a reasonable practice for many people and is often recommended for sustaining as a habit to experience various health benefits.

- Establishing a consistent sleep schedule is essential for overall well-being. It's beneficial to go to bed and wake up at the same time (or within a specific window) every day, aiming to get an early start in the morning. There are numerous advantages to rising early and commencing your day with physical activities such as walking, exercising at the gym, or practicing yoga. If time is limited, even simple stretching exercises can help activate your muscles. Engaging in body weight exercises like push-ups or squats can also be beneficial. Carving out just 15 minutes for stretching will not be difficult for most individuals. Waking up early allows you to align with the natural rhythms; the body's metabolic rate increases with the sunrise and decreases at sunset. Furthermore, waking up before the sun rises can assist in revitalising body cells, promoting a sense of rejuvenation.

- It's essential to prioritise getting a good 7 to 8 hours of uninterrupted sleep. Quality sleep can reduce the overall amount of time you need to sleep. Remember, the quality of your sleep is just as important for your body as eating nutritious food.

- I have heard that the body's natural repair processes for damaged cells are particularly active from 10 pm to 4 am. Therefore, maintaining a consistent sleep schedule, going to bed early, and rising before sunrise may support the body's recovery and overall health.

- Regular physical activity is essential; you should aim for about an hour daily. You can achieve this by incorporating various exercises such as taking a long brisk walk, running, engaging in strength training (such as weightlifting), or practicing yoga. To optimise your fitness routine, consider combining weight training and yoga. This combination will help build muscle strength while improving flexibility, contributing to overall physical well-being.

- The key goal is to keep your body consistently active throughout the day. It's essential to make an effort to move your body every two to three hours. Taking a moment to stretch every two hours can be highly beneficial. Regularly standing up from your chair every two hours and engaging in some form of physical activity, such as stretching your muscles, can make a significant difference. Also, consider sipping half a glass of water every two hours while incorporating a nice stretch. You can even perform stretching exercises while remaining seated in your chair. Activities such as getting up, walking to get water and hydrating yourself are also beneficial ways to stay active during the day.

It is well-established that maintaining a balanced and nutritious diet, engaging in regular physical activity, and getting adequate sleep are fundamental to living a healthy life. Taking care of our health is a personal responsibility and should be a top priority for everyone. Despite this, many overlook the importance of maintaining good health, citing life's uncertainties and a lack of discipline. They find numerous reasons for being unable to prioritise their physical and mental well-being. While I recognise that life is filled with uncertainties, I hold a different viewpoint when it comes to health. I firmly believe that regardless of life's duration, leading a physically fit and mentally resilient life is imperative.

It's important to remember that as we journey through life, there may be times when we need to make compromises or accept situations that are not at the level we had hoped for, whether it's in our professional, personal, or financial lives. However, it's crucial that we do not compromise on our overall well-being and health. Taking care of our physical fitness and overall health should be a top priority in our lives to ensure that we can lead fulfilling, satisfying, and long-lasting lives. Incorporating regular exercise, balanced nutrition, and mindful practices into our daily routines is essential to maintain our well-being and vitality.

Takeaways from Chapter-5

- Achieving and maintaining fitness doesn't have to be overly complicated. It boils down to incorporating healthy habits into our daily routines and prioritising our well-being.

- While both diet and physical activity are essential components of a healthy lifestyle, it's worth noting that our dietary choices contribute significantly to our overall fitness, accounting for approximately 80% of our fitness goals.

- Eating isn't just about satisfying hunger – it's about nourishing our bodies and understanding our consumption's impact on our health.

- Recognising the role of blood sugar and insulin is crucial for our overall well-being. The Glycemic Index is valuable in measuring how specific foods affect blood sugar levels.

- Opting for foods with a lower Glycemic Index, which leads to more stable blood sugar levels, can alleviate the body's need to produce excessive insulin to counteract high glucose levels.

- Our lifestyle and food choices may lead us to consume high-glycemic index foods, which can strain the pancreas by necessitating increased insulin release.

- It's important to note that artificially processed foods, packaged or canned drinks, and alcoholic beverages tend to rank high on the Glycemic Index.

- It's essential to be mindful of our eating habits in social gatherings, as excessive indulgence can lead to excessive calorie intake in a short period.

- Instead of constantly snacking, it's essential to establish specific eating and fasting times.

- By allowing our bodies time to undergo periods of fasting, we enable the cleansing process to occur.

- During fasting, the body utilises stored fats as its primary energy source once it has depleted available dietary carbohydrates (carbs), stored carbs (glycogen), and dietary fats.

- For fasting to be effective, it's recommended that you abstain from consuming any calorie for a minimum of 12 hours.

- Consuming various fruits and dried fruits can significantly benefit our health, thanks to their rich nutrient content, including vitamins, minerals, and fibre. However, being mindful of their natural sugar content is essential to maintain a balanced diet.

- When people consume calories equivalent to their Total Daily Energy Expenditure (TDEE), their body weight stays relatively constant.

- These maintenance calories serve as the baseline for determining the desired calorie intake needed to create a calorie deficit for weight loss or a calorie surplus for weight gain.

- Implementing intermittent fasting can be a beneficial strategy for reducing calorie intake. Limiting the feasting period to 8 to 10 hours each day provides individuals with a restricted window for consuming calories, which can aid in weight management.

- To minimise the potential adverse effects of social gatherings and parties, we must be mindful of our dietary choices before, during, and after attending these events.

- Physical activity prevents chronic diseases like heart disease, diabetes, and obesity. Additionally, it has been found to be significantly impacting mental well-being, enhancing cognitive functions and reducing stress.

- The connection between mental and physical health is intricate and vital for an individual's overall well-being.
- Effective communication can minimise the likelihood of conflicts and misunderstandings with others, positively impacting mental well-being.
- Prioritising our health over indulgences and luxuries is essential when it comes to fitness and physical activity.
- By prioritising health, we can lead fulfilling and healthy lives, promoting overall well-being.

CHAPTER 6

CONCLUDING CHAPTER

No One is Perfect

To date, I have not seen or heard of anybody who had a perfect life. Perfection is a myth. Imperfections, failures, bad decisions and bad experiences are part of everybody's life. We are all unique individuals with our own diverse range of intellectual and emotional capabilities. Our differences in intelligence quotient (IQ) and emotional quotient (EQ) contribute to the rich tapestry of human experience. We all live in different environments and are unique in some way or another, which is why our successes, failures, imperfections, decisions and experiences differ. We cannot copy a good part of anybody's life and paste the same into our lives.

Failures should not deter you. They are merely temporary pauses and not the end of life. Failing to achieve certain milestones should only indicate that either effort was insufficient or one is destined for something else. Even after failing, one can still improve one's life in many other areas.

The best thing we can do is observe how things happen in life and try to live positively. I know that you will live in a different environment compared to what I faced. This is why I have emphasised on basics and process. I did not give any readymade solution to live life or carve your life. I have tried to explain the complexities of life or common mistakes that we make in the initial years of work life or in general. Slip-ups and mistakes are bound to happen, so the best thing you can do is to **live life** consciously. **Don't live life accidentally**. As far as possible, Plan things, be it at work or home. Observe the lives of others and their mistakes and try not to repeat them. Make newer mistakes and learn from them so you don't repeat them. **Perfection is often seen as an ideal that is difficult to achieve, while the process is the practical and achievable path towards improvement**. In every aspect of life, it's essential to focus on the process rather than solely on the final results. When the process is well-planned and executed, the results will likely be positive, sooner or later.

No Cost Tips

Life offers countless ways to bring about positive change, many of which may come at a cost. However, without spending a penny, you can incorporate the following advice to add an extra sparkle to your life. I discovered these tips later in life, but they can be grasped at any time, ideally as early as possible. Not only will these tips bring about an extra sparkle, but they will also simplify your life in the long term.:-

- Every morning when you wake up, take a moment to appreciate the simple act of breathing and feel grateful for the gift of another day of life you've been given.

- When you start your day, take a moment to make your bed by neatly arranging the bed sheet and fluffing the pillows. This simple habit, taking just a minute of your time, has the potential to instill a sense of accomplishment and start your day with a positive mindset. Arranging your bedroom should be your responsibility.

- Getting into the habit of leaving the washroom clean and well-organised reflects good hygiene and shows respect for the next person who will use the facilities. This practice will make you a well-organised person.

- Make sure to keep your cupboard organised. Regardless of your financial status, it's essential to cultivate the habit of effectively managing and maintaining your own possessions independently.
- Always remember to be mindful of food wastage. Millions of people around the world don't have enough food to eat daily. Let's be grateful for having access to three meals daily and appreciate the privilege of never going hungry.
- Remember to be mindful of your eating habits. Your stomach belongs to you, so treat it with respect. Avoid overeating and consuming non-nutritious foods to maintain a healthy lifestyle. **Avoid letting your tummy become a garbage bin**.
- Remember to prioritise your health above everything else. Start by ensuring that your diet consists of nutritious and balanced meals that provide the essential vitamins and minerals to your body needs to function at its best. A balanced and wholesome diet that includes a variety of nutrients is essential for supporting cognitive function and maintaining consistent energy levels throughout the day. Additionally, aim for a consistent sleep schedule, as quality sleep is crucial for sustaining focus, alertness, and emotional well-being. Lastly, make daily physical activity a non-negotiable part of your routine to keep your body strong and healthy. Regular physical activity not only helps to alleviate stress but also enhances overall mood and mental clarity.
- Always remember to maintain this order of priority – food, sleep, and physical activity. These are the critical components of a healthy lifestyle.
- Make it a point to incorporate a daily habit of seeking new knowledge and skills. Embracing creativity is vital to stimulating and revitalising your body's neurons, which can spark motivation and inspiration.

- Make it a habit to read every day. Despite finding it uninteresting at first, you'll soon find it captivating and something you eagerly look forward to. One of the most effective ways to acquire knowledge and expertise is by immersing yourself in books and absorbing the wisdom from the experiences of others.

- Discipline is a timeless virtue that yields rich rewards when embraced in all areas of life. It never goes out of fashion. Whether it's maintaining professional standards, prioritising health and wellness, managing finances, or nurturing personal relationships, consistently adhering to discipline brings greater fulfillment and success. It's essential to approach all aspects of life with carefulness and commitment to reaping the benefits of a disciplined life.

- Each person is given the same 24 hours in a day, and it's essential to manage this time effectively to maximise productivity. Punctuality is the key, as it shows respect for your own time and that of others. It's critical to avoid wasting time and be mindful of how it impacts your life and those around you. When managing your tasks, it's essential to prioritise high-priority items to prevent last-minute stress. It's best to break large projects into smaller, more manageable tasks to make the overall project more feasible and less overwhelming.

- It is crucial to cultivate mental and physical resilience to navigate life's challenges as students or professionals. Life is unpredictable, and we are often faced with unfavourable circumstances. Developing a growth mindset allows us to perceive challenges as opportunities for growth. Reflecting on past experiences, learning from them, and making informed decisions based on that knowledge are essential aspects of personal and professional development. It is important to remain humble, prioritise continuous learning, and acknowledge that consistent effort plays a pivotal role in achieving success and progress.

- Creating a strong support system is crucial for maintaining overall well-being. It's essential to stay connected with family and friends through regular communication to receive emotional support. Additionally, collaborating with peers can provide mutual support and reduce feelings of isolation. Building a network of support contributes significantly to a sense of belonging and emotional stability.
- It's essential to avoid selfish behaviour in both professional and personal settings. Instead of pursuing targets solely for personal gain, it's better to consider the impact on others. It's essential to understand that nothing is permanent, so it's valuable to leave a positive legacy rather than be remembered for self-serving, self-centered actions.
- It is essential to take responsibility for yourself, your family, and your Nation. Feeling a sense of belongingness to your country will bring you happiness and pride. When citizens are responsible, they contribute to the greatness of the Nation.

Carving Your Life

Life is complex and multifaceted, much like a table with four legs. **These four legs represent different aspects of life, including work, marriage, finances, and fitness**. Balancing these four elements is crucial for a happy and fulfilling life. Each leg is equally essential for providing stability and support, and a well-rounded focus on all these areas can lead to a more harmonious and balanced life.

Understanding and maintaining balance in life requires focusing on four key aspects, which I refer to as the 'Legs' of a table. These four crucial elements encompass various facets of our lives, including personal, professional, physical, and emotional well-being. Often, we inadvertently neglect or prioritise one area over the others, leading to an imbalance that disrupts our overall harmony. Achieving balance involves nurturing each component equally to ensure fulfillment and security in all aspects of life.

It's crucial to recognise that it is absolutely okay to assert your boundaries and say 'NO' when the situation demands it. However, it's also essential to maintain an open mindset and be willing to tackle new challenges. When you establish yourself as someone who is firm and direct, others will respect your decisions. By doing so, they will have confidence in your affirmations (YES) and understand and appreciate your negatives (NO). Over-committing yourself can lead to burnout and disrupt the balance in various areas of your life. Therefore, it's crucial to establish clear boundaries in both personal and professional spheres. Setting and maintaining these boundaries, along with disciplined practices and efficient time management, can contribute significantly in addressing and overcoming life's various challenges.

To live a fulfilling life, it's essential to prioritise our physical, mental, and emotional well-being. By carefully defining our life priorities and goals, we can ensure that we make the most of our lives. Staying true to ourselves is the key to making everything possible. Always remember that we only have one life, and it is essential to be fully present and mindful in every moment of this life.

I found a beautiful quote about life that resonated with me: "**We all have one life, and if we live consciously, one is enough**." This quote reminds me to live life fully and appreciate every moment.

I am confident that the experiences and lessons I have gathered over the years will undoubtedly benefit not just you but many others as well. I have complete confidence in your ability to excel in all facets of life and to surpass my accomplishments. It is always a matter of joy and pride for any father when his son outgrows him in physical stature and exceeds his accomplishments. I would love to witness your personal growth and success. I want to experience the joy and pride of seeing you achieve great things and progress significantly. I wish you nothing but the best in all your endeavours. Please make sure to take good care of yourself, my dear son.

It's your birthday today. Happy 22nd birthday! May your special day be filled with love, joy, and unforgettable moments. I am wishing you tremendous happiness as you celebrate this milestone in your life.

Always keep yourself in high spirits and may good things come your way. I am always wishing the best for you.

Papa

----13 Jun 24/ 1630Hr----

ANNEXURE TO CHAPTER 5

Understanding your body's basal metabolic rate (BMR) is not just a theoretical concept, it's a practical tool for managing your health and fitness. By using the BMR formula, you can estimate your body's metabolism rate, which serves as a baseline for managing weight and calorie intake. This knowledge is not just for the health-conscious, but for anyone who wants to make informed decisions about their nutrition and exercise. Calculating BMR helps you understand your body's energy needs and plan appropriate nutrition and exercise regimens to achieve your health and fitness goals.

The body's unique metabolic rate, also known as the Basal Metabolic Rate (BMR), is influenced by various factors, including age, weight, height, gender, environmental temperature, dietary habits, and exercise routines. Once individuals have determined their BMR through online calculators or other methods, they can calculate their maintenance calories based on their activity level. BMR calculators are easily available on Google. One just need to fill age, gender, height and weight; and BMR can be obtained. The *Basal Metabolic Rate (BMR) Calculator*[xxiv] estimates your basal metabolic rate—the amount of energy expended while at rest in a neutrally temperate environment, and in a post-absorptive state (meaning that the digestive system is inactive, which requires about 12 hours of fasting).

Maintenance calories serve as the baseline for determining the desired calorie intake needed to achieve a calorie deficit for weight loss or a calorie surplus for weight gain. If you aim to increase your weight, you will need to consume more calories than your maintenance level, while the opposite is true for weight reduction. This process emphasises your role in managing your weight through calorie intake, making you feel responsible for your weight management.

Through BMR calculator, let's calculate maintenance calories for a boy who is 25 years of age, Weight 60 Kg, Height 180 Cm and performs moderate physical activity (1 to 3 times in a week).

BMR = 1,605 Calories/day

Maint Calories = 2207 Calories/day

Based on the figures provided, a 25-year-old male with specified parameters will have an approximate resting body calorie requirement of 1600 calories per day. With moderate physical activity, his daily calorie needs would be around 2200 calories per day. To lose weight, he would need to create a calorie deficit of 300-500 calories daily, meaning he should consume roughly 1700 to 1900 calories per day. On the other hand, if he wants to gain weight, he must consume 2500-2700 calories per day. This calorie consumption calculation is based on basic mathematics and is not overly complicated.

BMR Variables

Muscle Mass: Different types of exercises have varying effects on Basal Metabolic Rate (BMR). While aerobic exercises such as running or cycling do not directly impact BMR, anaerobic exercises like weight-lifting indirectly lead to a higher BMR by promoting the development of muscle mass. Greater muscle mass result in increased resting energy consumption, as more energy is required to sustain the body at rest. **Therefore, weight training burns more calories as compared to aerobic exercises.**

Age: Basal Metabolic Rate (BMR) tends to decrease with age. As an individual gets older, their BMR may lower, indicating a reduced minimum caloric intake required to maintain the functioning of their organs at rest. This decline in BMR with age can be attributed to factors such as muscle mass decreases and hormonal activity changes. **Therefore, one must reduce calorie intake with age**.

Genetics: Your genetic makeup can have a significant influence on your Basal Metabolic Rate (BMR). Factors such as body composition, metabolic efficiency, and hormonal balance, which are largely determined by your genes, can affect your baseline level of BMR. **Understanding this can help you make more informed decisions about your diet and exercise routine**.

Weather: The environment you're in can also affect your Basal Metabolic Rate (BMR). In cold environments, your body has to work harder to maintain a stable internal temperature, which can lead to a higher BMR. On the other hand, excessive heat can also increase BMR as your body tries to cool down. These are the body's natural adaptive mechanisms to maintain homeostasis, and **understanding them can help you better manage your energy expenditure**.

Diet: Dietary habits can influence BMR. Consuming small, frequent meals throughout the day can potentially increase BMR, while prolonged starvation or severely restricted caloric intake can decrease it. When the body experiences prolonged food scarcity, it may adjust its energy expenditure to conserve resources, reducing BMR. **Therefore, maintaining a disciplined eating time helps in maintaining BMR**.

Pregnancy: Pregnancy's metabolic demands can significantly raise the Basal Metabolic Rate (BMR). Internally supporting the growth and development of a fetus requires additional energy, leading to an increase in BMR among pregnant women. Hormonal changes during menopause can also impact BMR, leading to potential increases or decreases.

Supplements: Certain supplements and drugs can elevate BMR for various purposes, such as weight loss. Substances like caffeine stimulate the central nervous system, increasing BMR and potentially influencing energy expenditure.

Nutrition Calculation

I can give you a rough idea for calculating nutrition requirement of the body vis a vis calorie maintenance. As per ICMR (Indian Council of Medical Research) guidelines[xxv], an adult needs roughly 1 gm/ kg of body weight/ day protein. So, for a young boy of 60 kg weight, the protein requirement is 60 gm protein/ day. However, many athletes consume very high amounts of protein, often as protein powders. Protein requirements are lower than commonly perceived. Research findings indicate that dietary protein supplementation is associated with only a slight increase in muscle strength and size during prolonged resistance exercise training (RET) in healthy adults, and protein intake levels greater than ~ 1.6g/ kg/ day do not contribute any further to RET- induced gains in muscle mass.

So, a boy who is 25 years of age, Weight 60 Kg, Height 180 Cm and performs moderate physical activity (1 to 3 times a week) wants to reduce his weight without losing muscle mass would need to modify his diet as follows: -

BMR = 1,605 Calories/ day

Maint Calories = 2207 Calories/ day

He needs a calorie deficit of 300 to 500 Cal/ day for weight reduction. Let's take 300 Cal/ day for calculation purpose.

Calorie requirement per day = 2207-300 = 1907 Cal/ day $\simeq$ 1900 Cal/ day.

His protein intake should be 1.5 times of body weight = 60x1.5= 90 Gm/ day.

1 gm each of Protien, Fat and Carb gives the following calories:-

1 gm protein = 4 Cal

1 gm Fat = 9 Cal

1 gm Carb = 4 Cal

The boy will get 90x4 = 360 Cal from his protein intake.

Balance Calories left for the day = 1900-360=1540 Cal.

Approximately 20-25% Cal should come from Fat. i.e. 25% of 1540 = 385 Cal.

So, he can get 385/9= 42.7~ 43 gm fat per day.

Balance Calories left for the day = 1900-360- 385=1155 Cal.

He can get these calories from Carb, fruits and veggies.

Suppose he takes these calories from Carb. Then, he can take roughly 300 gm Carb daily (1155/4=288.75~300 gm).

Understanding the above calculation can help an individual effectively manage their daily energy requirements. While it may initially appear complex, once a person comprehends it and calculates their own energy needs, they can efficiently manage their energy consumption.

When considering our dietary choices, we must pay attention to the nutritional content of our foods (protein, fat, and carbs). Thanks to readily available resources like Google, we can easily access information about the nutritional value of various foods. While we don't need to obsess over calorie counting, it's crucial to be mindful of our overall eating habits and make health-conscious choices.

REFERENCES

[i] https://www.betterup.com/blog/what-is-ikigai

[ii] https://www.moneyseth.com/blogs/Fixed-Deposit-Interest-Rate-History-from-2000

[iii] https://www.thehindubusinessline.com/markets/gold/unlocking-wealth-analysing-niftys-journey-against-gold-over-20-years/article67689665.ece

[iv] https://www.nobroker.in/blog/house-price-graph/

[v] https://groww.in/p/government-bonds

[vi] https://economictimes.indiatimes.com/wealth/invest/mutual-fund-recommendations-14-6-category-average-returns-in-a-year-pick-highly-diversified-equity-funds/articleshow/105131220.cms?from=mdr

[vii] https://www.moneycontrol.com/mutual-funds/performance-tracker/returns/index-fundsetfs.html

[viii] https://www.thehindubusinessline.com/markets/gold/unlocking-wealth-analysing-niftys-journey-against-gold-over-20-years/article67689665.ece

[ix] https://www.livemint.com/money/personal-finance/finding-the-right-int-l-market-for-your-investments-11687105884592.html

[x] https://cleartax.in/s/lic-unclaimed-deposits

[xi] https://www.bankbazaar.com/home-loan-interest-rate.html

[xii] https://www.kotaksecurities.com/share-market/difference-between-large-small-mid-cap-in-share-market/

[xiii] https://kunaldesai.blog/nifty-50-cagr-last-20-years/

[xiv] https://www.thehindubusinessline.com/markets/gold/unlocking-wealth-analysing-niftys-journey-against-gold-over-20-years/article67689665.ece

[xv] https://www.otsuka.co.jp/en/health-and-illness/glycemic-index/glucose-level/

[xvi] https://www.mdpi.com/2072-6643/12/10/2989

[xvii] https://pgblazer.com/supplementary-action-of-proteins/

[xviii] https://www.who.int/news-room/fact-sheets/detail/obesity-and-overweight

[xix] https://www.quora.com/How-often-does-the-average-Indian-family-eat-out

[xx] https://www.healthline.com/nutrition/low-carb-ketogenic-diet-brain

[xxi] https://www.sciencedirect.com/topics/neuroscience/gluconeogenesis

[xxii] https://cleanhealth.edu.au/blog/wellness/understanding-maintenance-calories/

[xxiii] https://www.healthline.com/health/what-is-basal-metabolic-rate

[xxiv] https://www.calculator.net/bmr-calculator.html?ctype=metric&cage=49&csex=m&cheightfeet=5&cheightinch=10&cpound=160&cheightmeter=180&ckg=88&cmop=0&coutunit=c&cformula=m&cfatpct=20&x=Calculate

[xxv] https://main.icmr.nic.in/sites/default/files/upload_documents/DGI_07th_May_2024_fin.pdf

www.ingramcontent.com/pod-product-compliance
Lightning Source LLC
LaVergne TN
LVHW041705070526
838199LV00045B/1206